PENGUIN CLASSICS

ON ARGENTINA

JORGE LUIS BORGES was born in Buenos Aires in 1899 and was educated in Europe. One of the most widely acclaimed writers of our time, he
published many collections of poems, essays, and short stories before his
death in Geneva in June 1986. In 1961, Borges shared the International
Publisher's Prize with Samuel Beckett. The Ingram Merrill Foundation
granted him its Annual Literary Award in 1966 for his "outstanding con-
tribution to literature." In 1971, Columbia University awarded him the
first of many degrees of Doctor of Letters, *honoris causa* (eventually the
list included both Oxford and Cambridge), that he was to receive from
the English-speaking world. In 1971, he also received the fifth biennial
Jerusalem Prize and in 1973 was given one of Mexico's most prestigious
cultural awards, the Alfonso Reyes Prize. In 1980, he shared with Gerardo
Diego the Cervantes Prize, the highest literary accolade in the Spanish-
speaking world. Borges was director of the Argentine National Library
from 1955 until 1973.

ALFRED MAC ADAM has been a professor of Latin American literature
at Barnard College and Columbia University since 1983. He previously
taught at the University of Virginia, Yale University, and Princeton University. His area of specialization is twentieth-century Latin American
narrative, a subject on which he has published three books and numerous
articles. Mac Adam is also a translator of Latin American fiction and has
translated novels by Carlos Fuentes, Mario Vargas Llosa, José Donoso,
Alejo Carpentier, Reinaldo Arenas, Julio Cortázar, Juan Carlos Onetti,
and Osvaldo Soriano. He also translated from the Portuguese Machado
de Assis's *The Immortal* as well as a selection of Fernando Pessoa's *Book
of Disquiet*. Mac Adam edited *Review: Latin American Literature and
Arts*, a publication of the Americas Society, from 1984 until 2004.

SUZANNE JILL LEVINE, the distinguished translator of such innovative Spanish American writers as Manuel Puig, Guillermo Cabrera
Infante, Jorge Luis Borges, and Julio Cortázar, is the author of *The Sub-
versive Scribe: Translating Latin American Fiction* and *Manuel Puig and
the Spider Woman: His Life and Fictions*. A professor of Latin American
literature and translation studies at the University of California at Santa
Barbara, she has been awarded PEN American Center and PEN USA
West awards, National Endowment for the Arts and for the Humanities
grants, and a Guggenheim Foundation fellowship.

JORGE LUIS BORGES

On Argentina

Edited with an Introduction and Notes by
ALFRED MAC ADAM

General Editor
SUZANNE JILL LEVINE

PENGUIN BOOKS

PENGUIN BOOKS

Published by the Penguin Group

Penguin Group (USA) Inc., 375 Hudson Street, New York, New York 10014, U.S.A.

Penguin Group (Canada), 90 Eglinton Avenue East, Suite 700, Toronto, Ontario, Canada M4P 2Y3
(a division of Pearson Penguin Canada Inc.)

Penguin Books Ltd, 80 Strand, London WC2R 0RL, England

Penguin Ireland, 25 St Stephen's Green, Dublin 2, Ireland (a division of Penguin Books Ltd)

Penguin Group (Australia), 250 Camberwell Road, Camberwell, Victoria 3124, Australia
(a division of Pearson Australia Group Pty Ltd)

Penguin Books India Pvt Ltd, 11 Community Centre, Panchsheel Park, New Delhi–110 017, India

Penguin Group (NZ), 67 Apollo Drive, Rosedale, North Shore 0632, New Zealand
(a division of Pearson New Zealand Ltd)

Penguin Books (South Africa) (Pty) Ltd, 24 Sturdee Avenue, Rosebank, Johannesburg 2196, South Africa

Penguin Books Ltd, Registered Offices: 80 Strand, London WC2R 0RL, England

First published in Penguin Books 2010

Some of the selections were published in Jorge Luis Borges's *Obras completas*.
© Maria Kodama and Emece Editores S.A., 1989.

Translations of "Man on Pink Corner" and "The South" are reprinted from *Collected Fictions* by Jorge
Luis Borges, translated by Andrew Hurley (Viking Penguin). Copyright © Penguin Group (USA) Inc.,
1998. Translations of "Our Inabilities," "I, a Jew," "Definition of a Germanophile," "Our Poor
Individualism," and "The Argentine Writer and Tradition" are reprinted from *Selected Non-Fictions* by
Jorge Luis Borges, edited by Eliot Weinberger and translated by Esther Allen, Suzanne Jill Levine, and
Eliot Weinberger (Viking Penguin). Copyright © Penguin Group (USA) Inc., 1999.

Alastair Reid's translations of "The Mythical Founding of Buenos Aires" and "General Quiroga Rides to
His Death in a Carriage," are reprinted from *Selected Poems 1923–1967* by Jorge Luis Borges, edited by
Norman Thomas Di Giovanni (Delacorte Press, 1972) and his translation of "Truco" (poem) is reprinted
from *Selected Poems* by Jorge Luis Borges, edited by Alexander Coleman (Viking Penguin, 1999).
By permission of Alastair Reid.

LIBRARY OF CONGRESS CATALOGING IN PUBLICATION DATA
Borges, Jorge Luis, 1899–1986.
[Essays. English. Selections]
On Argentina / Jorge Luis Borges : edited with an introduction and notes by Alfred Mac Adam.
p.   cm.—(Penguin classics)
"The twenty selections chosen for this collection will flesh out the vision of the young Borges between
1925 and 1930. These essays constitute an important intellectual biography of one of the most
influential Latin American authors of all time"—Provided by the publisher.
ISBN 978-0-143-10573-2
1. Borges, Jorge Luis, 1899–1986—Translations into English.
I. Mac Adam, Alfred J., 1941–   II. Title.
PQ7797.B635A22   2010b
864'.62—dc22   2010010824

Set in Adobe Sabon

146028962

To the memory of Emir Rodríguez Monegal and John Alexander Coleman. *I primi lumi.*

Contents

Introduction

NINETEEN-HUNDRED-TWENTY-SOMETHING

The circular path of the stars is not infinite
And the tiger is one of the forms that return,
But far from chance and adventure, we
Thought we were exiled to an exhausted time,
Time when nothing can happen.
The universe, the tragic universe, was not here
And we had to look for it elsewhere;
I plotted a modest mythology of adobe walls and knives
And Ricardo thought about his cowhands.

We had no idea the future contained the lightning bolt,
We had no foreboding about shame, fire, the monstrous
     night of the Alliance;
Nothing told us that Argentine history would
     stalk the streets,
History, indignation, love,
The masses like the sea, the name of Córdoba,
The taste of the real and the incredible, the horror
     and the glory.

Jorge Luis Borges (1899–1986) published this poem in his wistful 1960 collection of short prose pieces and poems, *El hacedor* [*Dreamtigers*]. Like so many works in that book, it concerns memory. The sixty-year-old, increasingly sight-impaired author thinks over his past, even the tigers that populate his poetry and turn up in the conclusion of his self-destroying essay "A New Refutation of Time" (1946). The poem recollects and reconstructs his (and his friends') state of mind in the early 1920s. But Borges is as selective about what he culls from memory here as he is in his "Autobiographical Essay," first published in *The New Yorker* in 1970, which conceals more than it reveals.

The Borges family had definitively moved back to Buenos Aires following a seven-year European sojourn between 1914 and 1921. These were the war years, which they spent in Geneva, and the years immediately following, which they spent in Spain. (The family's 1923–24 visit to Europe was just that, a visit made without any thought about remaining forever in the Old World, a genuine possibility earlier.)

"Nineteen-Hundred-Twenty-Something" reconstructs the provincial despair of a young, polyglot, *au courant* Argentine freshly back from Europe. The stodginess and cultural barrenness of Buenos Aires, as Borges wrote in 1960, led him to delve into local mythology ("adobe walls and knives"), and this resulted in the essays he published during the 1920s about Argentina, his obsession. Fourteen of those early essays, later repudiated by their author, are included here, along with six later pieces that chronicle Borges's continuing fascination with his homeland. The anthology ends in 1951, with his magisterial lecture "The Argentine Writer and Tradition," in which he finally discovers the link between local and universal culture.

Between 1924 and 1930, Borges was desperately casting about for a means to create a modern Argentine literature, as if speculating about it could make it appear, as if those speculations might be more valid than his forays into the avant-garde in *Ultraísmo*.[1] What his 1960 poem about the period does not do is reflect accurately the Argentina the Borges family found on its return. That is, the culturally stultifying ambience (the "time when nothing can happen") Borges depicts is by no means a complete picture of Argentina in 1925, when he published his first collection of essays, *Inquisiciones*. Argentina emerged unscathed from World War I and apparently in excellent condition. The nation was able to lend France money, certainly a point of pride for a developing country whose upper classes adored French culture. But even this could not mask the contradictions of Argentina's reality, that it was at war with itself. All of the social and political inequities that plagued Argentina after independence in 1810 remained unresolved and were compounded by a massive influx of immigrants.

Hipólito Irigoyen (1852–1933) and his Radical Party came

into office (1916) with a popular mandate: to wrest economic control from the landowning oligarchy and reform the state economically and politically. This Irigoyen failed to do, and the Tragic Week (Semana Trágica) of January 1919 (news of which may well have prompted the Borges family to postpone its return to Buenos Aires) rang with violent clashes between Anarchist unions and the police, skirmishes that ultimately stimulated the formation of the ultra-right-wing Liga Patriótica, which attacked Jews simply for being Jews.

Borges suggests he and his generation were adrift, that he became interested in local themes out of a kind of anguish and that neither he nor his friends (the Ricardo of the poem would seem to be Ricardo Güiraldes, author of the 1926 novel *Don Segundo Sombra*) had any idea what the future had in store for them. He then compresses Argentine history and leaps ahead to the 1960s and 1970s, referring to the Cordobazo, the 1968 uprising of workers and intellectuals in the city of Córdoba and the arrival of the murderous Alianza Anticomunista Argentina (or AAA) that attacked left-wing *peronistas* and others whom they perceived to be on the left during the 1970s. Borges emphasizes the "rebellion of the masses," or as he puts it, "Nothing told us that Argentine history would stalk the streets." In fact, however, the Argentine masses had become a factor in Argentine life by the time of the Semana Trágica. The truth is, the city Borges and his family returned to in 1921 was the capital of a nation racing toward disaster.

Why Borges would turn to local mythology is a complex matter—not simply a matter of personal desperation. Borges began reading Oswald Spengler in 1924,[2] and in his 1926 essay on W. H. Hudson's *The Purple Land*, he twice refers to *The Decline of the West* (1918), a major influence on non-European intellectuals, who read it as a death sentence for European cultural preeminence. Spengler's theory of the biological nature of cultures—their having a birth, a maturation, and a death—would appeal to the young Borges, who had a very good idea of the destruction wrought in Europe by World War I. Like many intellectuals in Russia and elsewhere in Latin America, he thought it was now the time for the periphery, in his case

Argentina, to step forward on the world cultural stage. This passage from "The Complaint of All *Criollos*" (1925), a summary of Argentine history, contains a heavy dose of Spenglerian thought as well as a surprisingly militaristic prognostication:

> Rosas's quiet misgovernment is gone: the railroad made land valuable; miserable and profitable agriculture impoverished easy cattle ranching; and the *criollo*, transformed into a foreigner in his own land, understood in sorrow the hostile meaning of the words "Argentinity" and "progress." . . . They bear the blame for the barbed wire fences that incarcerate the pampa, for the fact that gaucho life has collapsed, that the only profession for *criollos* is the army or unemployment or the underworld, that our city is called Babel. . . . In Hernández's poem and in Hudson's bucolic narratives . . . are the first acts of the *criollo* tragedy. The last acts are yet to come. . . . The Republic is becoming foreign to us. . . . The *criollo* is failing, but he is also becoming arrogant just as the fatherland is growing insolent. There are flags in the wind; perhaps tomorrow by virtue of killings we'll intervene to civilize the continent. We shall be a strong nation. . . . Dying is the destiny of races and individuals. You have to die well . . . and with a nice joke on your lips. The example of Santos Vega comes to mind. . . . To die singing.

This rambling passage summarizes the young Borges's fatalistic vision of Argentine history, especially the idea that the *criollo* will disappear in the same way the gaucho disappeared. Borges links the gaucho past to the *criollo* present through literature: *Literatura gauchesca* (exemplified here by Hilario Ascasubi's character Santos Vega) becomes elegiac in Borges's reading, and he seems to have conceived his particularly *porteño* vision of *criollo* culture as a means to preserve the memory of that culture.

The passage also raises, without alluding to them openly, family-related reasons for Borges's obsession with Argentina. He cannot escape his family's links with the nation's past and the process of Spanish American independence: His maternal great-grandfather, Isidoro Suárez (1799–1847), led the charge at the battle of Junín (1824), where the Spanish Army was defeated. His mother's family were fervent *unitarios* and had nothing but contempt for Argentina's nineteenth-century dictator, Juan Manuel de Rosas (1793–1877), leader of the *federales*. Partly as a reaction against his overweening mother and partly because he admired Rosas's virile *criollo* personality, Borges extolled the tyrant as the true spirit of the nation. That the masses came to identify Rosas with Juan Domingo Perón (1895–1974), Argentina's twentieth-century tyrant and Borges's nemesis, is certainly one of the ironies history was preparing for the Borges of the 1920s. The link between Rosas and Perón would be obvious, for example, in 1970, when all over Buenos Aires signs proclaiming QUEREMOS LOS RESTOS DE ROSAS (We want the remains of Rosas) were a demand for the return and restoration of Perón, which took place in 1973.

There are other reasons: Borges grew up in the seedy Palermo district of Buenos Aires and had firsthand knowledge of street-corner thugs (*compadritos*) and the tangos that accompanied them. He had to balance that urban vision against the fact that Argentina's literary past began with the siege of Montevideo (1843–1852), carried out by Rosas. It was then that educated *porteño* intellectuals wrote satiric poems in the vernacular of the gaucho soldiers. Borges's challenge was to discover a way to bring the rustic charms of *poesía gauchesca* into the seething urban reality of Buenos Aires.

There can be no doubt that James Joyce's *Ulysses*, whose last page he translated and about which he wrote an essay in 1925 (included in *Selected Non-Fictions*), was a huge influence: If Joyce, on the Irish periphery of British culture, could create the quintessential modernist literary text and also minutely re-create the city of Dublin, why couldn't Borges do the same for Buenos Aires? The fatal difference between Borges and Joyce is obvious: In 1925, Argentina was a peripheral culture, as was Joyce's Ireland, but where Joyce could look with resentment and admiration toward London's thriving culture market, Borges could do no such thing with regard to Madrid. There is a fallacy at the heart of the comparison Borges was silently forging.

Yet another reason why Borges turned to local subjects was his xenophobia. The Argentine culture he tried to galvanize between 1925 (*Inquisiciones*) and 1930 (*Evaristo Carriego*) is not that of the millions of immigrants who had flooded the nation since the nineteenth century, but that of the *criollos*, Argentines nominally descended from Spaniards. By 1925, they were a minority in their own nation. He doggedly stuck to this task until politics caught up with him and obliged him to understand that *criollos* were insignificant as heirs to an Argentine cultural heritage and that the nation was in perilous condition because the immigrant masses had yet to be assimilated into the political structure of the nation, and had yet to be given their full rights as citizens.

The crisis broke on September 6, 1930, when the army, under General José F. Uriburu, effected its first Argentine coup d'état of the twentieth century. The next decade would be the chronicle of the steady rise to power of the populist, pro-fascist Juan Domingo Perón, who capitalized on the disenfranchised state of the immigrant masses to carry out his political agenda. In 1946, with Perón now president of Argentina, Borges suffered humiliation. In his "Autobiographical Essay," he observes:

> In 1946, a president whose name I do not want to remember came to power. One day soon after, I was honored with the news that I had been "promoted" out of the library [the Miguel Cané Library in the lower-class neighborhood of Almagro, where he'd worked since 1938] to the inspectorship of poultry and rabbits in public markets.

Whether Borges was actually transferred to the department of *avicultura,* or poultry (the rabbits are his own addition) or, as some Peronist functionaries claimed, the department of *apicultura,* or beekeeping, the fact is that the transfer was the kind of insult the thin-skinned Borges was unlikely to ignore. Borges resigned from the public payroll and began earning a living as a lecturer. Perón had made Borges a stronger man.

Borges's essays from the 1920s assembled here all deal with the language, literature, and music of Argentina and, more specifically, Buenos Aires. We have Borges the reader of *poesía gauchesca*, Borges the avant-garde manifesto writer, Borges the ideologue of *criollo* culture, Borges the young poet worshipping at the altar of local minor poetic deities like Almafuerte and Evaristo Carriego, Borges extolling the virtues of slim talents like Pedro Leandro Ipuche, and a Borges who feels he can set the record straight about the origins of the tango.

The second, disillusioned phase of Borges's meditations on Argentina begins with "Our Inabilities"(1931). Here Borges refers to *criollos* as if the species had virtually disappeared and was only to be found in its pristine state "in Uruguay's northern provinces." Even the *porteño* he dismisses for his "lack of imagination" and his "resentment." At the end of this bitter and sardonic essay, Borges notes: "I have been an Argentine for many generations and express these complaints with no joy." "I, a Jew" (1934) complements Borges's now ironic attitude toward Argentina by pointing out that the ultra–right-wing magazine *Crisol* [Crucible] accused him of secretly being a Jew, but that despite his hopes that the accusation might be true he is unfortunately not one, that Argentine anti-Semites can't even identify their enemies correctly.

There would seem to be no hope for Borges's recovering his faith in Argentina, but "The Argentine Writer and Tradition" is exactly that. Borges settles his account with his own past exaltation of the *criollo*:

> [I]n books now fortunately forgotten, I tried to compose the flavor, the essence, of the outskirts of Buenos Aires; naturally I abounded in local words such as *cuchilleros*, *milonga*, *tapia,* and others, and in such manner I wrote those forgettable and forgotten books; then, about a year ago, I wrote a story called "Death and the Compass," . . . a nightmare in which elements of Buenos Aires appear. . . . [A]fter the story was published, my friends told me that at last they had found the flavor of the outskirts of Buenos Aires in my writing.

Re-creating the local through local words, which is what Borges falsely calls his attempt to construct a *criollo* aesthetic, is indeed a dead end, but the essays gathered here from the 1920s remind us there was more to *criollismo* than local color. Borges ends this lecture with a hope that turns out to be a prediction:

> I believe that Argentines, and South Americans in general . . . can take on all the European subjects, take them on without superstition and with an irreverence that can have, and already has had, fortunate consequences. . . . [W]e must believe that the universe is our birthright and try out every subject; we cannot confine ourselves to what is Argentine in order to be Argentine because either it is our inevitable destiny to be Argentine, in which case we will be Argentine whatever we do, or being Argentine is a mere affectation, a mask.

From a man who in 1925 felt he could only speak to *criollos* about *criollismo*, Borges evolves into one who understands that, like the Faulkner he admired, he can be both local and universal at the same time, that literary expression is a matter of discovering a personal vernacular and allowing the spirit of the age to express itself in it. That his essay is both an homage to and a parody of T. S. Eliot's 1919 article "Tradition and the Individual Talent" renders it not only an exhortation to all Latin American writers but an enactment of the very doctrine it preaches.

ALFRED MAC ADAM

NOTES

1. All Spanish-language terms like this one are either defined or elucidated in the glossary.
2. The mountainous Borges bibliography makes reading him seriously a daunting project. Solid biographies like Edwin Williamson's *Borges: A Life* (2004) are invaluable vademecums for anyone interested in Borges's life and work.

A Note on the Text

This anthology supplements the 1999 *Selected Non-Fictions* volume edited by Eliot Weinberger. Weinberger found himself in a quandary: Borges wrote so many essays over his long career, covering so many topics, that the editor would have to make some compromises just to keep things manageable. Weinberger, as he says in his introductory note, assembled a selection "for the English-language reader" (xv) and perforce had to exclude essays that might seem to speakers of English of purely local interest. Of the twenty-two articles assembled in this edition, six derive from Weinberger's collection: They document Borges's escape from the parochialism of his youth and his mature linking of Argentina to universal culture. The other sixteen seek to inform the English-speaking reader about Borges's life-long obsession with Argentina—its tango, its card games, its politics, and its literary history.

The early essays, published between 1925 and 1928, are from books Borges actually destroyed whenever possible: His "complete works" are anything but complete. His reasons for expunging these texts are complex, but these are two likely possibilities: In these essays, Borges desperately tries to emulate in writing the intonations of Argentine Spanish. He uses local expressions and phonetically reproduces oral pronunciation (*criolledá* instead of *criolledad*). He then weds this artificially vernacular prose to an avant-garde modality that abuses neologisms. The result is a spiky, hard-to-understand Spanish that Spanish American readers today find impenetrable. The mature Borges was simply embarrassed by such excesses. The second possible reason is that to be young is often to be tendentious, as is evident here in Borges's savage review of Leopoldo Lugones, a writer he came to revere and to whom he dedicates his 1960 book *El hacedor* [*Dreamtigers*]. While Borges's chagrin is understandable, his efforts in these early pieces provide an invaluable guide to his youthful thinking. They also resoundingly belie all theories of Borges as a cosmopolitan mind without a country. No Argentine subject is alien to him, although he does conspicuously avoid discussing the plastic arts, which is bizarre given that his beloved sister Norah was a painter. Perhaps the visual arts were of little interest to him.

The reader will note that some of the terms Borges uses repeatedly have been left in Spanish. To translate them would mean finding English equivalents for purely Argentine concepts. I have therefore included them, along with names of people and places, in a glossary. My hope is that by doing so, the reader gets a feel for Borges's original terminology. Translating Borges's early work is difficult: His style is tortuous, his vocabulary rarified, and his focus is often blurred by ambiguous metaphors. The choice between providing a literal translation—thus producing an incomprehensible text—and rendering his prose in plain English was difficult. Ultimately, we came down on the side of moderate infidelity, producing texts that readers could not only understand but enjoy. (I would like to acknowledge my debt to Suzanne Jill Levine for her help with the translation. She spearheaded this enterprise, and it was only through the force of her energy that it was brought to completion. Thanks also to Jessica Powell for her editorial assistance.)

Most of the essays in this volume are my translations, and are followed by the attribution [AMA] at the end of each essay. Other translations were contributed by Esther Allen [EA], Andrew Hurley [AH], Suzanne Jill Levine [SJL], Alastair Reid [AR], and Eliot Weinberger [EW].

The anthology also contains three poems and two fictions. The reasons for including these nonessayistic creative pieces is to show how organic Borges's thinking was throughout his career. To write an essay on the card game *truco* and to write a poem on the same subject were natural to him, and for this reason there are many similarities between the lyric and the essay. Similarly, the fictions that appear here reflect Borges's ideas about Argentine culture at the time he wrote them. Thus, "Man on Pink Corner" exactly replicates Borges's idealization of street-corner thugs, his love of the tango, and his fascination with vernacular heroism. "The South" is in many ways an auto-biographical tale (like its protagonist Juan Dahlmann, Borges suffered a life-threatening infection in 1938) and reflects the author's attitude toward Argentine violence. Where he'd ideal-ized the virility of Juan Manuel de Rosas (whose trademark color was red) and extolled his brutal leadership, Borges through Dahlmann depicts himself as a victim of that cult of savagery. Yes, Juan Dahlmann accepts a challenge that he knows will kill him, and yes, he does so because he'd rather die that way than lying in a hospital bed, but the fact is that there is no glory in his death. It is suicide, the same kind committed by Facundo Quiroga in Borges's poem about him, "General Quiroga Rides to His Death in a Carriage," with an Argentine twist. Again, any anthology is an arbitrary selection: Our hope with this one is to create a vision of Borges that corresponds more closely to reality.

ALFRED MAC ADAM

On Argentina

MAN ON PINK CORNER

For Enrique Amorim

Imagine you bringing up Francisco Real that way, out of the clear blue sky, him dead and gone and all. Because I met the man, even if this wa'n't exactly his stomping ground—his was more up in the north, up around Guadalupe Lake and Batería. Truth is, I doubt if I crossed paths with the man more than three times, and all three were on a single night—though it's not one I'll be likely ever to forget. It was the night La Lujanera came home to sleep at my place—just like that, just up and came—and the same night Rosendo Juárez left Maldonado never to return. Of course you probably haven't had the experience you'd need to recognize that particular individual's name, but in his time Rosendo Juárez—the Sticker, they called him—was one of the toughest customers in Villa Santa Rita. He was fierce with a knife, was Rosendo Juárez, as you'd expect with a moniker like that, and he was one of don Nicolás Paredes's men—don Nicolás being one of Morel's men. He'd come into the cathouse just as dandified as you can imagine, head to foot in black, with his belt buckle and studs and all of silver. Men and dogs, both, had a healthy respect for him, and the whores did too; everybody knew two killings'd been laid to him already. He wore a tall sort of hat with a narrow brim, which sat down like this on a long mane of greasy hair. Rosendo was favored by fortune, as they say, and we boys in the neighborhood would imitate him right down to the way he spit. But then there came a night that showed us Rosendo Juárez's true colors.

It's hard to believe, but the story of that night—a night as strange as any I've ever lived through—began with an insolent red-wheeled hack crammed with men, banging and rattling along those streets of hard-packed clay, past brick kilns and vacant lots. There was two men in black, strumming guitars and lost in their own thoughts, and the man on the driver's seat using his whip on any loose dogs that took a mind to mess with the piebald in the traces, and one fellow wrapped tight in a poncho riding in the middle—which was the Yardmaster that everybody always talked about, and he was spoiling for a fight, spoiling for a kill. The night was so cool it was like a blessing from heaven; two of these fellows were riding up on the folded-back cloth top of the hack—and it was as though the loneliness made that rattletrap a veritable parade. That was the first event of the many that took place, but it wa'n't till a while afterward that we found out this part. Me and my friends, meantime, we'd been over at Julia's place since early that evening, Julia's place being a big old barracks-like building made out of sheets of zinc, between the Gauna road and the Maldonado. It was a place you could pick out from quite a distance off, on account of the light from a brazen big red light—and on account of the hullabaloo too. This Julia, although she was a colored woman, was as reliable and honest as you could ask for, so there wa'n't ever any lack of musicians, good drinks, and girls that could dance all night if they was asked to. But this Lujanera I mentioned, who was Rosendo's woman, she outdid 'em all, and by a good long ways. La Lujanera's dead now, señor, and I have to admit that sometimes whole years go by that I don't think about her, but you ought to have seen her in her time, with those eyes of hers. Seein' her wouldn't put a man to sleep, and that's for sure.

Rotgut, milongas, women, a *simpático* kind of curse at you from the mouth of Rosendo Juárez, a slap on the back from him that you tried to feel was friendly-like—the truth is, I was as happy as a man could be. I was paired up with a girl that could follow like she could read my mind; the tango was having its way with us, whirling us this way and then that and losing us and calling us back again and finding us. . . . To make a long story short, we boys were dancing, 'most like bein' in a dream, when all of a sudden the music seemed to get louder, and what it was was that you could begin to hear the guitar strumming of those two fellows I mentioned, mixing in with the music there at Julia's, and coming nearer every minute. Then the gust of wind that had brought it to us changed direction, and I went back to my own body and my partner's, and the conversations of the dance. A good while later, there came a knock at the front door—a big knock and a big voice, too. At that, everybody got still; then a man's chest bumped the swinging doors open and the man himself stepped inside. The man resembled the voice a good deal.

For us, he wa'n't Francisco Real yet, but you couldn't deny he was a tall, muscular sort of man, dressed head to foot in black, with a shawl around his shoulders about the color of a bay horse. I remember his face being Indian-like, unsociable.

One of the swinging doors hit me when it banged open. Like the damn fool I am, I reached out and swung at the fellow with my left hand while with my right I went for the knife I kept sharp and waiting in the armhole of my vest, under my left arm. If we'd've tangled, I wouldn't have lasted long. The man put out his arm—and it was all he had to do—and brushed me aside, like he was brushing away a fly. So there I was—half sprawled there behind the door, with my hand still under my vest, holding on to my useless weapon, while he just kept walking, like nothing had happened, right on into the room. Just kept walking—taller than any of the boys that were stepping aside to make way for him, and acting like we were all invisible. The first row of fellows—pure Eye-talians, an' all eyes—opened out like a fan, and fast. But that wa'n't about to last. In the pack just behind those first fellows, the Englishman was waiting for him, and before that Englishman could feel the stranger's hand on his shoulder, he floored him with a roundhouse he had waitin'—and no sooner had he landed his punch than the party started in for serious. The place was yards and yards deep, but they herded the stranger from one end of it to the other, bumping him and shoving him and whistling and spitting. At first they'd hit him with their fists, but then when they saw that he didn't so much as put up a hand to try to block their punches, they started slapping him—sometimes with their open hands and sometimes just with the harmless fringe on their shawls, like they were makin' fun of him. And also like they were reserving him for Rosendo, who hadn't budged from where he was standing, back against the back wall, and without saying a word. He was taking quick puffs of his cigarette—I will say that—like he already had an inkling of what the rest of us would see clear enough later on. The Yardmaster—straight and bloody, and the wind from that jeering mob behind him—was getting pushed and shoved back to Rosendo. Whistled at, beaten, spit on, as soon as he came face to face with Rosendo, he spoke. He looked at him and he wiped off his face with his arm, and he said this:

"I'm Francisco Real, from up on the Northside. Francisco Real, and they call me the Yardmaster. I've let these poor sons of bitches lift their hands to me because what I'm looking for is a man. There are people out there—I figure they're just talkers, you know—saying there's some guy down here in these boondocks that fancies himself a knife fighter, and a bad 'un—say he's called the Sticker. I'd like to make his acquaintance, so he could show me—me being nobody, you understand—what it means to be a man of courage, a man you can look up to."

He said that, and he never took his eyes off him. Now a sticker for real glinted in his right hand—no doubt he'd had it up his sleeve the whole time. All around, the fellows that had been pushing to get close started backing away, and every one of us was looking at the two of them, and you could have heard a pin drop. Why, even the black gentleman that played the violin, a blind man he was, he had his face turned that way.

Just then I hear movement behind me, and I see that in the doorway there's standing six or seven men, which would be the Yardmaster's gang, you see. The oldest of them, a weather-beaten, country-looking man with a gray-streaked mustache, steps forward and stands there like he's dazzled by all the women and all the light, and he very respectfully takes his hat off. The others just stood there watching, keeping their eyes open, ready to step in, you see, if somebody wanted to start playing dirty.

Meantime, what was happening with Rosendo—why hadn't he come out slashing at that swaggering son of a bitch? He hadn't said a word yet, hadn't so much as raised his eyes. His cigarette, I don't know whether he spit it out or whether it just fell out of his face. Finally he managed to get a few words out, but so quiet that those of us down at the other end of the room couldn't hear what he was saying. Then Francisco Real called him out again, and again Rosendo refused to rise to the occasion. So at that, the youngest of the strangers—just a kid he was—he whistled. La Lujanera looked at him with hate in her eyes and she started through that crowd with her braid down her back—through that crowd of men and whores—and she walked up to her man and she put her hand to his chest and she pulled out his naked blade and she handed it to him.

"Rosendo, I think you're needing this," she said.

Right up next to the roof there was this long kind of window that looked out over the creek. Rosendo took the knife in his two hands and he seemed to be trying to place it, like he didn't recognize it. Then all of sudden he reared back and flung that knife straight through the window, out into the Maldonado. I felt a cold chill run down my spine.

"The only reason I don't carve you up for beefsteak is that you make me sick," said the stranger. At that, La Lujanera threw her arms around this Yardmaster's neck, and she looked at him with those eyes of hers, and she said, with anger in her voice:

"Forget that dog—he had us thinking he was a man."

Francisco Real stood there perplexed for a second, and then he put his arms around her like it was going to be forever, and he yelled at the musicians to play something—a tango, a milonga—and then yelled at the rest of us to dance. The milonga ran like a grass fire from one end of the room to the other. Real danced straight-faced, but without any daylight between him and her, now that he could get away with it. They finally came to the door, and he yelled:

"Make ways, boys—she's gettin' sleepy!"

That's what he said, and they walked out cheek to cheek, like in the drunken dizziness of the tango, like they were drowning in that tango.

I ought to be ashamed of myself. I spun around the floor a couple of times with one of the girls and then I just dropped her—on account of the heat and the crowdedness, I told her—and I slunk down along the wall till I got to the door. It was a pretty night—but a pretty night for who? Down at the corner stood that hack, with those two guitars sitting up straight on the seat, like two Christian gentlemen. It galled me to see those guitars left out like that, to realize that those boys thought so little of us that they'd trust us not even to walk off with their cheap guitars. It made me mad to feel like we were a bunch of nobodies. I grabbed the carnation behind my ear and threw it in a mud puddle and then I stood there looking at it, more or less so I wouldn't have to think of anything else. I wished it was already the next day, so I'd have this night behind me. Just then, somebody elbowed me, and it felt almost like a relief. It was Rosendo, slipping through the neighborhood all by himself.

"Seems like you're always in the way, asshole," he muttered as he passed by me—I couldn't say whether to get it off his chest or because he had his mind on something else. He took the direction where it was darkest, down along the Maldonado; I never saw the man again.

I stood there looking at the things I'd been seeing all my life—a sky that went on forever, the creek flowing angry-like down below there, a sleeping horse, the dirt street, the kilns—and I was struck by the thought that I was just another weed growing along those banks, coming up between the soapworts and the bone piles of the tanneries. What was supposed to grow out of trash heaps if it wa'n't us?—We was big talkers, but soft when it came to a fight, all mouth and no backbone. Then I told myself it wa'n't like that—the tougher the neighborhood, the tougher a man necessarily had to be. A trash heap?—The milonga was having itself a ball, there was plenty of racket in the houses, and the wind brought the smell of honeysuckle. The night was pretty, but so what? There were enough stars that you got dizzy lookin' at 'em, one on top of another up there. I struggled, I tell you, to make myself feel like none of what had happened meant anything to me, but Rosendo's turning tail, that stranger's insufferable bullying—it wouldn't let me alone.

The tall son of a bitch had even gotten himself a woman for the night out of it. For that night and many more nights besides, I thought to myself, and maybe for all the rest of his nights, because La Lujanera was serious medicine. Lord knows which way they'd gone. But they couldn't be far. Probably at it hammer and tongs right now, in the first ditch they'd come to.

When I finally got back inside, that perfectly pleasant little dance was still going on, like nothing had ever happened.

Making myself as inconspicuous as I could, I peered around through the crowd, and I saw that one and another of our boys had slipped out, but the guys from the Northside were tangoing along with everybody else. There was no elbowing or words or anything; everything was real polite, but everybody was keeping their eyes open. The music was kind of sleepy, and the girls that were dancing with the Northside boys were as meek as mice.

I was expecting something, but not what turned out to happen.

Outside we heard a woman crying, and then a voice that was familiar in a way, but calm, almost *too* calm, as though it didn't belong to a real person, saying to her:

"Go ahead, darlin', go on in," and then some more of the woman's crying. Then the voice seemed to be getting a little desperate.

"Open the door, I said! Open the door, you motherless bitch, open the door!"

At that, the rickety doors swung open and La Lujanera stepped in, alone. She came in kind of looking over her shoulder, like somebody was herding her inside.

"She's got a spirit back there commanding her," said the Englishman.

"A dead man, my friend," said the Yardmaster then. His face was like a drunkard's. He came in, and he took a few unsteady steps into the clearing that we all made for him, like we had before. He stood there tall, and unseeing, and then he toppled like a post. One of the boys that had come with him turned him over on his back and put his poncho under his head for a pillow. The boy's hands came away bloody. That was when we saw that he had a big knife wound in his chest; his blood was pooling up and turnin' black this bright red neckerchief he was wearing, but that I hadn't noticed before because his shawl had covered it. To try to stop the blood, one of the girls brought over some rotgut and scorched rags. He was in no condition to tell us what'd happened, and La Lujanera was looking at him sort of vacant-like, with her arms just hanging down at her sides. Everybody was asking her what happened with their eyes, and finally she managed to find her voice. She said that after she'd gone outside with the Yardmaster there, they went off to a little vacant lot, and just then a stranger appeared and desperately called out the Yardmaster to fight, and he stabbed him, gave him that wound there, and she swore she didn't know who the man was, but it wa'n't Rosendo.

Who was going to believe that?

The man at our feet was dying. My thought was, whoever had fixed his clock, his hand had been pretty steady. But the Yardmaster was tough, you had to give him that. When he came to the door just now, Julia had been brewing up some *maté*, and the *maté* went around the room and came all the way back to me before he was finally dead. "Cover my face," he said, when he knew he couldn't last anymore. His pride was all he had left, and he wa'n't going to let people gawk at the expressions on his face while he lay there dyin'. Somebody put that high-crowned black hat over his face, and he died under it, without a sound. When his chest stopped rising and falling, somebody got up the nerve to uncover him—he had that tired look that dead men get. He was one of the toughest men there was back then, from Batería to the Southside—but no sooner was he dead and his mouth shut for all time, I lost all my hate for him.

"All it takes to die is to be alive," one of the girls back in the crowd said, and then another one said something else, in a pensive sort of way:

"Man thought so highly of himself, and all he's good for now is to draw flies."

At that, the Northsiders all muttered something to each other, real low, and then two of 'em at the same time said it out loud:

"The woman killed 'im."

One of 'em yelled in her face, asking her if it was her that did it, and they all surrounded her. At that I forgot all about being meek and not getting in anybody's way, and I pushed through to her like a shot. I'm such a damn fool, it's a wonder as mad as I was I didn't pull out the little dagger I always carried on me. I could feel almost everybody—not to say everybody—looking at me.

"Look at this woman's hands," I said with a sneer. "Do they look steady enough—does she look like she'd have heart enough—to put a knife in the Yardmaster like that?"

Then I added, cool but tough at the same time:

"Who'd've thought the dear departed, who they say was a man to be reckoned with on his own turf, would've ended up this way, and in a backwater as dead as this is, where nothin' ever happens unless some strangers wander in to give us somethin' to talk about and stay around to get spit on afterward?"

Nobody rose to that bait, either.

Just then through the silence came the sound of riders. It was the police. For one reason or another, everybody there had reason to keep the law out of this, so they decided that the best thing was to move the body down to the creek. You'll recall that long window that the gleam of the knife sailed through? Well, that's the very same way the man in black went. A bunch of them lifted him up and after they'd separated him from all the money and whatnot he had on him, somebody hacked off his finger to get to the ring he wore. Vultures, señor, to pick over a poor defenseless dead man like that, after another, better man has fixed 'im. Then a heave-ho, and that rushing, long-suffering water carried him away. I couldn't say whether they gutted him—I didn't want to look. The gray-mustached individual never took his eyes off me. La Lujanera took advantage of all the shuffling about to disappear.

By the time the law came in to have their look around, the dance had a pretty good head of steam up again. The blind man on the violin knew how to play habaneras the likes of which you won't hear anymore. Outside, the day began to want to dawn a little. There was a line of arborvitae posts along the top of a hill, standing there all alone-like, because you couldn't see the thin strands of wire between 'em that early in the morning.

I strolled nice and easy on home to my place, which was about three blocks away. There was a light burning in the window, but then it went out. When I saw that, I can tell you I moved a good bit faster. And then, Borges, for the second time I pulled out that short, sharp-edged knife I always carried here, under my vest, under my left arm, and I gave it another long slow inspection—and it was just like new, all innocent, and there was not the slightest trace of blood on it.

[1935]   *[AH]*

FROM

INQUISITIONS

(1925)

BUENOS AIRES

Not by morning light, not when day has come, and not even at night do we really see the city. Morning is an overwhelming blue, a swift and massive surprise spanning the sky, a crystallizing, a lavish outpouring of sunlight that piles up in squares, smashes mirrors with fictitious stones, and lowers long insinuations of light down wells. The day is a playing field for our endeavors or for our idleness, and there is only room for them on their usual chessboard. The night is a truncated miracle: the crowning moment of wan streetlights, when palpable objectivity becomes less insolent and less solid. The dawn is an infamous, dragged-out affair, because it conceals the great plot arranged to set right everything that fell apart ten hours before. It goes about straightening streets, decapitating lights, and repainting colors exactly where they were the previous afternoon. Finally, we—with the city already hanging on our necks and the abyssal day yoked to our shoulders—have to give in to the mad plenitude of its triumph and resign ourselves to having yet another day riveted to our souls.

Now for the afternoon: the dramatic altercation and conflict between the visible and the shadows. It's as if visible things begin twisting, going insane. Afternoon weakens us, eats away at us, abuses us, but because of its persistence the streets recover their human meaning, their tragic meaning of volition that manages to last in time, time whose very essence is change. The afternoon perturbs the day, and for that reason it agrees with us, because we too are perturbed. The late afternoon prepares the easy decline of our spiritual electricity. It's by force of afternoons that the city goes about entering us.

Despite the transitory humiliation some eminent buildings manage to inflict on us, the total vision of Buenos Aires has nothing vertical to it. Buenos Aires is not a raised-up, ascendant city that disturbs the divine limpidity with the ecstasy of assiduous towers or a smoky mob of busy chimneys. Rather, it is a replica of the flatness that surrounds it, and the submissive straightness of that plane continues in the straightness of streets and houses. Horizontal lines overwhelm vertical lines. Perspectives—on one- or two-story dwellings lined up and facing one another all along the miles of asphalt and stone—are so easy that they don't seem improbable.

Four infinities meet at every crossroad. Late at night, walking the city that hard shadows and our grumbling surrender simplify, we have at times become uneasy seeing the interminable streets that cross our path, and we become dazed, stabbed, or rather, lanced, and even shot up by the distance. And when it's just coming on to twilight! Gigantic sunsets take place that incite the depth of the street to riot and barely fit in the sky. In order for our eyes to be flagellated by them in the full force of their passion, we have to seek out the *arrabales* that oppose their scantiness to the pampa.

In the face of that indecisive part of the city, where the final houses take on a reckless character, like aggressive beggars facing up to the enormity of the absolute and scorched plain, the sunsets, like astounded, upright ships, parade by. People who've lived in the mountains can't imagine those shocking sunsets, like raptures of the flesh, and more impassioned than a guitar. Sunsets and visions of the suburb that are still—pardon my pedantry—in their aseity (their underived, independent existence), since the aesthetic disinterest of the *porteño arrabales* is an extremely well-known fabrication among us. I, who have straightened out my verses to contradict that lie, know too much about the deviation that everyone shows praising the torn beauty of such banal places. . . .

A few lines back, I mentioned houses. They constitute the most moving element in Buenos Aires. So pitifully identical, so isolated in their extremely narrow crowding, so unique in their doors, so petulant with their railings and marble thresholds, they simultaneously declare their timidity and their pride. There's always a patio on one side, a poor patio that never has a fountain and almost never has a vine or well, but which is full of patrician spirit and primitive efficacy because it's founded on the two most primordial things that exist: earth and sky.

These houses I'm talking about are the translation into plaster and brick of the spirit of their inhabitants. They express fatalism. Not the rancorous, anarchic fatalism wielded in Spain, but the mocking, *criollo* fatalism that shapes the *Fausto* of Estanislao del Campo and the stanzas of the *Martín Fierro,* not humiliated by the prejudices of cheap liberal doctrine. A fatalism that does not stop action, but which sees failure on the fringes of all effort . . .

I also want to talk about plazas. And in Buenos Aires, the plazas—noble basins overflowing with coolness, congresses of patrician trees, settings for romantic meetings—are the unique havens where for an instant the streets give up their persistent geometric nature and break ranks. They scatter away running, like people after a riot. If the houses of Buenos Aires are cowardly statements, the plazas are a declaration of momentary nobility given to all the passersby they shelter.

Houses of Buenos Aires roofed with red-tiled or zinc *azoteas,* lacking exceptional towers and resolute eaves, comparable to tame birds with clipped wings. Streets of Buenos Aires made profound by a transitory barrel organ, vehement public expression of our souls; delightful streets, sweet in the enjoyment of memory, long like waiting; streets where hope, the memory of that which is to come, strolls; streets nailed together and solid so forever in my desire. Streets that approach silently with the noble sadness of being *criollo.* Streets and houses of the homeland. If only I can live the days to come in your bountiful intimacy.

[1921]   [AMA]

THE MYTHICAL FOUNDING OF BUENOS AIRES

And was it along this torpid muddy river
that the prows came to found my native city?
The little painted boats must have suffered the steep surf
among the root-clumps of the horse-brown current.

Pondering well, let us suppose that the river
was blue then like an extension of the sky,
with a small red star inset to mark the spot
where Juan Díaz[1] fasted and the Indians dined.

But for sure a thousand men and other thousands
arrived across a sea that was five moons wide,
still infested with mermaids and sea serpents
and magnetic boulders that sent the compass wild.

On the coast they put up a few ramshackle huts
and slept uneasily. This, they claim, in the Riachuelo,
but that is a story dreamed up in the Boca.
It was really a city block in my district—Palermo.[2]

---

1 Juan Díaz de Solís was an explorer who rowed into the River Plate in 1516 and was promptly devoured by Indians. [AR]

2 Palermo is a district in the city of Buenos Aires, originally the Italian quarter, where Borges spent his childhood. [AR]

A whole square block, but set down in open country,
attended by dawns and rains and hard southeasters,
identical to that block which still stands in my neighborhood:
Guatemala—Serrano—Paraguay—Gurruchaga.

A general store pink as the back of a playing card
shone bright; in the back there was poker talk.
The corner bar flowered into life as a local bully,
already cock of his walk, resentful, tough.

The first barrel organ teetered over the horizon
with its clumsy progress, its habaneras, its wop.
The cart-shed wall was unanimous for YRIGOYEN.[3]
Some piano was banging out tangos by Saborido.

A cigar store perfumed the desert like a rose.
The afternoon had established its yesterdays,
and men took on together an illusory past.
Only one thing was missing—the street had no other side.

Hard to believe Buenos Aires had any beginning.
I feel it to be as eternal as air and water.

[1929]

[AR]

3 Irigoyen (Hipólito Irigoyen, 1852–1933) was the twice-elected president of
Argentina and victim of a military coup in 1930. [AR]

ASCASUBI

There is delight in efficacy: in love, when it is the glory of two entwined bodies and wills; in red sunsets announcing the afternoon's perdition; in language, when it inscribes its signature on the spirit. All intensity is plausible, but there is also pleasure in irresolution: in loves that don't dare become passion; in the routine of ordinary days that oblivion will efface and whose features will, over time, become vague; in sentences that are barely possible and do not ignite a fire in souls. The untidy pleasure Ascasubi has supplied to my curiosity belongs in that category.

His *Santos Vega* is the totality of the pampa. The interminable adventures he narrates could take place anywhere (more to the west, more to the south, where that inviting road begins, behind that dust cloud), adventures that are unaware of one another like the disconnected incidents in a dream. His rhythm is indolent and very relaxed: a rhythm of lazy days no clock could ever measure, days that harmonize better with the quadruple march of the prolix seasons and the almost immobile time governing the placid duration of trees. His pulse is the pulse of memory. We know that while Ascasubi began his writing in Uruguay in 1850, he only managed to finish it off (in both senses of the term) in Paris when he'd reached the homey, downhill slopes of a chatty, melancholy old age.

As we read him, the slack and negligent plot of the blessed story escapes us more than once, and we take note only of the narrator's tone. The tone of an old gentleman who carefully pronounces words and in whose darkened drawing room an honorable sword rusts away. The tone of a gentleman of the *Unitario* party in whom survive poignant words from the deceased *criollo* lexicon and stiff metaphors like *the bitter bread of exile* and *the altar of the fatherland*. And all that expressed on lofty occasions. In his daily life I see him as a devil, full of wit, full of grave *criollo* sarcasm, capable of talking his way through a game of *truco* with slow efficacy and of reaching and deserving any man's friendship.

A few lines back I said about his most important work that it was blurred and hazy like a daydream. The few passages that contradict my assertion already appear in anthologies. There is a depiction of the dawn in which well-known gaucho charm and unforeseen Spanish charm combine felicitously:

> The light of dawn
> brightened the sky
> and the fluttering chickens
> dropped to the ground
> from the branches . . .
>
> And the cattle, bedazzled,
> stumbled toward the corral;
> it was nice entertainment
> to see *a venteveo*
> perched on a bull, singing away.
>
> The beast seems to take pleasure in the song
> because he calmly keeps his ears erect
> as if he doesn't want
> to scare the bird away . . .
>
> And the ponies mingling
> with the mares whinnied,
> and hidden in the distance
> the restless mustangs answered.

Equally famous is his hallucinatory description of the hostile Indian raid, when, aside from the Indian horde, we have the forbidding and vast attack of the pampa itself with its vermin, its wind, and its savage moons:

But when the Indian horde invades you feel it
because out of the heart of the pampa the animals
flee out of fright:
tangled in vines
come wild dogs,
foxes, ostriches, lions,
bucks, hares, and does;
afflicted, they pass
right through the settlements.

Then the sheep dogs
chase wildly through
and also the lapwings
flutter about screaming.
But, this for sure:
the first who announce the news
with all certainty
when the Pampa Indians attack
are the *chajás* that
screech as they fly: *chajá! chajá!*

Equally worthy is the picture of an impenetrable sky black-
ened by storm clouds at dawn, with its slippery setting and the
whinnying of the lost horses along the wooded banks of a great
muddy river.

The three cantos that open the poem are also tremendously
pleasing and carved from clear peace. Insuperable is his depiction of a singer who goes from ranch to ranch and who pays
back the hospitality offered him by filling with words the at-
tentive simplicity of those idle afternoons, unfolding long narratives that are sinuous and primitive and as loose as a lasso in
the air. The Santos Vega those cantos promise seems to over-
come Martín Fierro through the spontaneity of his performance
and the absence of protest or complaint. It's unfortunate that
the later chapters do not fulfill that promise and depress it in
jokes, invariably poor and never elevated by the manly friendship that gives shape to parallel scenes in the *Fausto*. This is
where we see Ascasubi's defects: He leads the way with his

eventual discoveries to the two artistic works that derive from his plain style and whose jubilant branches pour a funereal shadow over him.

That is also his glory. The creations of Estanislao del Campo and Hernández were only possible because of their precursor Ascasubi. Estanislao del Campo honored himself in manifesting his debt. We see him express how much he owes Ascasubi in his pseudonym and in a letter he published in *La Tribuna* (see the edition of *Santos Vega* published by La Cultura Argentina, p. 19) as well as in an extremely pretty poem that Calixto Oyuela transcribes.

How is Ascasubi's work different from that of his followers? It's the difference between unbeauty and beauty. An insuperable abyss, if we follow the superstition of the cultured elite or the vanity of romantic enthusiasts. The abyss becomes a docile shade for the sincere artisan who confesses his obligation to study models and wear disguises and whose disillusionment smacks of the gunpowder and sulphur that are the true splendor in the skyrocket.

It's difficult to invent a form and the beauty of that form at the same time, as Alain argues (*Propos sur l'esthétique*, p. 103). A vulgar criterion concedes preeminence to the one who takes a form and makes it profound. Another, making the opposite mistake, ascribes preeminence to the initiator.

All art is a preestablished custom of expressing beauty. Gaucho poetry, perhaps born in Uruguay with the ballads of Hidalgo, later wandered gloriously along our side of the river with Ascasubi, Estanislao del Campo, Hernández, and Obligado. Now it closes its great cycle in the voices of Pedro Leandro Ipuche and Fernán Silva Valdés.

[1925]   [AMA]

THE *CRIOLLO* ELEMENT
IN IPUCHE

The domain of *gauchesco* art has always been the banks of the Plata, and the unnamed river is like a harmonious heart within its body of classical stanzas, which know nothing of alien flora but do speak of a tree, the *ombú,* and a kind of grass, the *flechilla.* Already in the nineteenth century, the pampa pronounced its primitive, pastoral heroic verse in Ascasubi's poem—his chatty mockery in the *Fausto*—and in the premonition of a death in the adventures of the *Martín Fierro.* Today the Uruguayan hills, the *cuchillas,* are filled with song. On this side, the only poetry from whose depth the entire pampa arises like a tide is that controlled by Ricardo Güiraldes. On the other bank we have Fernán Silva Valdés and Pedro Leandro Ipuche.

Fernán Silva Valdés's poetry comes chronologically later than Ipuche's compositions, and also incarnates a later phase of *criollo* consciousness. The *criollo* element in Silva Valdés is already immobilized in symbols and its language, too conscious of its individuality, and allows no foreign terms. Ipuche's *criollo* side is a living thing that merges with others. Gaucho language in his diction is yet another virtue, and the subjects he treats are not necessarily local. Moreover, among the country themes, he usually concedes preeminence to those that legend has not rendered prestigious. His greatest decorum is rhythm, and his forceful skill in herding migrating verses, as well as his inevitable rectitude, like a fast river that flows within, all make us proud.

The other efficacies in his manly diction—thoughtful use of

adjectives, proper use of tropes, and charm as a narrator—all speed helter-skelter along the surface of the illustrious impetuosity of his words. This omnipotence of rhythm is a true index of the strong popular strain in his work. Andalusian lyric is no different: So silent in terms of images, it is generous in strophic configurations and has pluralized its voice in typical Andalusian melodies like the *soleá* and the *soleariya*, in joyous gypsy quatrains and those seven-verse stanzas, the *seguidillas*.

There is in Ipuche a Pan-inspired sense of the forest. *Tierra honda* [Deep Land] is the title of his best book, and the epithet speaks of feeling rooted and tied to the living land, of sinking sweet and desiring roots into the native land. I once applied the adjective *honda* (deep) to the city, thinking about those long streets that stretch beyond the horizon along with the outlying slums that grow more impoverished as they extend and crumble to shreds into the afternoon. But in Ipuche's mouth the word *honda* means something very different, an almost physical feeling for the land, somber beneath wandering steps. He brings to life in words a hard-working and primordial existence. That awareness of an enjoyable disorder receives its most explicit realization in *Poemas de la luz negra* [Poems of the Dark Light], and it always reminds me of Lucretius's line in which the image of mating branches recalls that other image of bodies lustfully entwined:

Tunc Venus in sylvis jungebat corpora amantum.[1]

Ipuche is no atheist even if in the *Poems of the Dark Light* he expands the operative presence that, as theologians put it, pertains to God in the world, in essential presence. He approaches pantheism. His figuration of God as light appears in the Manicheans, who also dissolved the divinity in a resin of souls and called the moon and sun lucid ships.

Ipuche is a notable fan of dialogue and, especially, of friendly emulation and companionship and of the common accord with

---

1 Then in the forest Venus joined the loving bodies. [AMA]

which freewheeling individuals help one another. There are few compositions of his that my heart hasn't felt. Today my gratitude wants to point out the singular gifts I've received from "El corderito serrano" [The Lamb from the Hills], "Mi vejez" [My Old Age], "La clisis" [The Crisis], "El caballo" [The Horse], "Correría de la bandera" [Attack of the Flag], and "Los carreros" [The Cart Drivers]. His poetry is one of total virility: It speaks of God and men and has seen itself in the festive faces of human friendship and in the great moon of solitary meditation.

A final acknowledgment: I spoke of the gift of joy with which some stanzas of *Tierra honda* deified my bosom. I want as well to admit an embarrassment. Reciting his words I have trembled at length out of nostalgia for the countryside, and I have suffered the shame of my vague urban nature whose native fiber is (barely!) a noble sadness in the face of the reproach from desiring guitars or in the presence of that urgent and subtle arrow reserved for us in old-fashioned entranceways in whose depth the patio is as limpid as a fresh rose.

[1924]   [AMA]

THE COMPLAINT OF
ALL *CRIOLLOS*

Nations show two faces: one, the obligatory, conventional face, formulated according to the requirements of the age and, most often, following the prejudice of some famous definer. The other, true and beloved, defined by slow history, manifests itself through language and customs. Between those two images, the apparent and the essential, we usually detect a notorious contradiction. Take the Cockneys of London. Without a doubt the most reverent, submissive, and featureless people I've ever seen in my travels, but Dickens celebrates them for being impudent and quick-witted, qualities that, if they ever had them, they do no longer. But every English writer maintains the lie with lax tenacity.

With regard to Spaniards, we all agree these days (advised by Romantic literature and simply noting their history, their conquest of the New World, and what they did on Dos de Mayo 1808 [May 2nd], when they rose up against Napoleon) about the unbridled vehemence of their character without recalling that Baltasar Gracián formulated an antithesis between Spanish indolence and French impetus. I offer these two examples so the reader's judgment will be inclined to agree with what he may find odd in my assertion.

I want to stress the overwhelming dissimilarity between the *criollo's* true character and the one people want to inflict on him.

To my way of thinking, the *criollo* is a joker, distrustful, disillusioned beforehand about everything, and with such little stomach for verbal grandiosity that he only tolerates it in a few and celebrates it in none. The marriage of silence and fatalism is beautifully incarnated in the two great leaders who embraced the soul of Buenos Aires: Rosas and Irigoyen. Don Juan Manuel, despite his crimes and the blood he uselessly spilled, was much loved by the people. Irigoyen, despite official hypocrisy, is forever governing us.

What people appreciated in Rosas, understood in Roca, and admire in Irigoyen is their condemnation of theatrics or their carrying it out with mockery. . . . In nations whose people are more life-loving, famous leaders seem foolish and exaggerated in their gestures, but here they are taciturn and almost apathetic. Verbal immodesty would take away the advantage of such fame. Our lack of enthusiasm is so deeply rooted that it even turns up in our history—a chronicle of workers, not thinkers. San Martín disappearing at Guayaquil; Quiroga heading for a trap—composed of inevitable and accurate daggers—out of pure, boastful fatalism; Saravia, contemptuous of an easy and victorious entry into Montevideo: All exemplify my assertion.

However, history is not the best place to trace the outlines of a people's spiritual face. . . . A noble artistic instinct, a tenacious absence of the ways tragedy brings resolution, causes all historians to take notice of the irregularity of a riot rather than calm and quiet decades of a daily routine. Political alternatives are also an influence. Future ups and downs determine if it's better to attribute some greater reality to Liniers's protest or to the ruckus of an open town meeting.

Let us consider some other aspect that's more common: for example, our *criollo* poetry. It has both tranquility and disillusionment; it is simultaneously harsh and saccharine. Spanish style on the other hand is pure vehemence: You might say that upon settling here, that vehemence dissipated, got lost out on the pampa. Speech acquired a drawl, the identical nature of all horizons frustrated ambition, and the obligatory rigor of subjugating a savage world rewarded itself in the sweet languor of contrapuntal *payadas*, of joking bouts of *truco*, and of *maté*. Castilian intensity relaxed, but among the *criollos* that smiling fatalism remained steadfast and lively, the very fatalism that enabled the two best works of Hispanic literature—Cervantes's

Quixote in prose and Francisco de Quevedo's *Moral Epistle* in poetry: two exaltations of failure.

Suffering, bland nostalgia, malicious and calm mockery are the eternal themes of our popular poetry. There is no shocking display of metaphors in that verse. Attempts at metaphor never come to fruition. The common folk song called *vidalitá* says, "There is no branch in the wild, *vidalitá*," the similarity between the heart wounded by absence and the forest mistreated by the severe winter is never established, but we have to catch a glimpse of it if we want to comprehend the stanza. The efficacy of gaucho-style verses is not achieved through ostentatious display, doesn't reside in the *ictus sententiarum*, the final push of declarations, as Seneca would put it, but in the easy linking of the totality:

> Just look at the ponies. Look at those guys!
> Two sovereign mounts.
> As if they were brothers
> Drinking water together.

murmurs Estanislao del Campo with light-handed perfection. The same happens in the *Martín Fierro*. The verbal austerity of stanzas like the following is very moving:

> There was a little Italian captive
> Who was always talking about the ship
> And they drowned him in a puddle
> For having caused the plague.
> He had blue eyes
> Like a pinto colt.

Just as significant is the modesty Martín Fierro exercises while experiencing great anguish over the death of his comrade. Rather than locate it in his tale, he prefers to shunt it off to the past:

> On my knees at his side
> I commended him to Jesus.

> Darkness covered my eyes,
> I fell as if struck by lightning.
> I felt a terrible fainting
> When I saw Cruz dead.

In the absurd anonymous couplets strummed out from guitar to guitar, everything idiosyncratic about the *criollo* element manifests itself. The Andalusians achieve comedy by means of pure nonsense and hyperbole; the *criollo* achieves it by frustrating an expectation, promising the listener a continuity he suddenly cuts short:

> Gentlemen, listen to me:
> I once had a colt
> Who on one flank was dapple-gray
> And on the other as well.

> On the bank of a little creek
> I saw two bulls drinking.
> One was red
> And the other . . . took off running.

> When the partridge sings
> Clouds are on the way;
> There's no better sign of water
> Than when it rains.

Martín Fierro is also rich in examples of frustrated contrast:

> Out of others come rhymes
> Like water out of a spring;
> Well, the same thing happens to me.

Sadness, motionless mockery, ironic insinuation: these are the only sentiments a *criollo* art can express without a foreign accent. Lugones is excellent in "El solterón" [The Old Bachelor] and "Luna quimera" [Lunar Chimera], but his grandiloquence as a yawn-inspiring shocker of readers is terrible. With regard to loudmouths like Ricardo Rojas, made of foam, patriotic blather, and unfathomable nothingness, they are a paradoxical debasement of our true way of being. The public feels it and, without bothering to make judgments about his work, prudently sets it aside, assuming, and rightly so, that it is more grand than legible. No one would dare think that Fernández Moreno is more worthy than Lugones, but our Argentine soul is in better accord with the serenity of the former than with the latter's arduous Gongoresque baroque.

Lugones, in an obviously apprenticelike relationship with Herrera y Reissig or Laforgue and in a cautious apprenticelike relationship with Goethe, is the least lamentable example of our situation today: that of the *criollo* trying to decriollize himself in order to conquer this century. His tragic dilemma is ours, his triumph, the exception to many failures.

Rosas's quiet misgovernment is gone: The railroad made land valuable; miserable and profitable agriculture impoverished easy cattle ranching; and the *criollo*, transformed into a foreigner in his own land, understood in sorrow the hostile meaning of the words "Argentinity" and "progress." No prolix cabalistic enumerator of letters has displayed before any word the reverence that we allot to those two. They bear the blame for the barbed wire fences that incarcerate the pampa, for the fact that gaucho life has collapsed, that the only profession for *criollos* is the army or unemployment or the underworld, that our city is called Babel.

In Hernández's poem and in Hudson's bucolic narratives (written in English, but more our own than any sorrow) are the first acts of the *criollo* tragedy. The last acts are yet to come, and their stage will be the enduring plain and linear vision of Buenos Aires, disturbed by mobility. The Republic is becoming foreign to us; we are losing it. The *criollo* is failing, but he is also becoming arrogant just as the fatherland is growing insolent. There are flags in the wind; perhaps tomorrow by virtue of killings we'll intervene to civilize the continent. We shall be a strong nation. By virtue of military nobility, our great men will shine in the eyes of the world. They will have to be invented if they don't exist. There will also be rewards for the past. Let's

hope, reader, that they recall you and me in that proper distri-
bution of glory.

Dying is the destiny of races and individuals. You have to die
well, without too much insistence or complaint, without pretending that the world is losing its sap for that reason, and with
a nice joke on your lips. The example of Santos Vega comes to
mind, and with a remaining admonishment I had not previously
detected: To die singing.

[1925]   [AMA]

EDUARDO GONZÁLEZ
LANUZA

It's essential we draw a sharp and deep distinction between the intimate intentions that motivated *Ultraísmo* in Spain and those that caused it to produce in these parts bright blossoms, some scattered and others gathered up in books. *Ultraísmo* in Seville and Madrid was a desire for renewal, the desire to delineate the time of art with a new cycle. It was, you might say, a lyric written in big red letters on the pages of the calendar whose salient emblems—planes, antennas, and propellers—register a chronological actuality.

Ultraísmo in Buenos Aires was the desire to achieve an absolute art that would not depend on the unfaithful prestige of voices and that would last in the perpetuity of language like a certainty of beauty. Under the energetic clarity of streetlamps, the names of Huidobro and Apollinaire were frequently heard in cenacles. Meanwhile, we, mobile and serious under the suburban stars, were scrutinizing lines from Garcilaso, seeking a limpid art that might be as atemporal as those perennial stars. We abominated the blurred colors of *Rubendarismo*, but we were emboldened by metaphor, because of its inherent precision, because of its algebraic way of linking distant things.

Among us, no one was as vehement in his fervor as González Lanuza. To our small group of *criollos*, apathetic and mocking, González Lanuza contributed a robust, Cantabrian joy, a red happiness like those of the drums and fifes and burning logs of a Saint John's Day bonfire. His enthusiasm was as fast-flowing as a mountain river. I published *Prisma* with him—the first, only, and ineffective mural magazine—and it was his voice that suggested, as dawn was breaking, that we paste a copy on the moon, big and vacant at the moment and at ground level. . . .

Since that yesterday, three years have passed. Today, González Lanuza published the book of poems that motivates this examination. I've read his admirable verses, I've savored the sweet gentleness of his music, I've duly felt the grandeur of some metaphors, but I've also noted that, unintentionally, we've all indulged in another rhetoric as linked as the ancient ones to verbal prestige. Our poetry, whose flight we judged loose and assured, has been tracing a geometric figure in the air of time. It's a beautiful but sad surprise to realize that our gesture back then, so spontaneous and easy, was nothing more than the awkward beginning of a liturgy.

All of *Ultraísmo*'s motifs are woven together with insistent purity in the volume I'm speaking about. All the Faustian words that attempt to capture distance and whose mere enunciation is memorable for the bleeding of time, are omnipotent in him. The sunset that is never among us but in heaven; the cry that symbolizes the pain of the ephemeral, just as the irrevocable kiss symbolizes its grace; silence, which is pure negation transformed into charm. The sunset that refers doubly to a spatial distance and to a loss of hours; the bird and its flight, which are the same fugitive thing transformed into a symbol, are engraved on each of his pages.

González Lanuza has composed the exemplary book of *Ultraísmo* and has drawn a winding path of our unanimous feelings. His book, poor in personal intentions, is archetypal in terms of a generation. The other recent hymnals simply do not deserve that name. In Guillermo de Torre's *Propellers*, the mischievous quality of his misanthropic lexicon gets in the way; in Maples Arce's *Interior Scaffolds*, it's his mockery; in Reyes's *Drunken Boat*, it's the preponderance of the sea motif; in the complex clarity of *Image* by Diego, the exacerbated devotion to Huidobro; in Bernárdez's *Kindergarten*, the puerile brevity of emotion; in Fernán Silva Valdés's wild and noble *Water of Time*, the primacy of gaucho subjects; and in my *Fervor of Buenos Aires*, a long-lasting metaphysical disquiet. González Lanuza has achieved our book, the book that is our deed in time and our defeat in the absolute. Defeat, because usually no moving intuition vivifies his metaphors; a true accomplishment because the replacement of the luxurious words of *rubenismo* with those of distance and desire produces, as far as today is concerned, a thing of beauty.

[1924]   *[AMA]*

FROM

MOON ACROSS THE WAY

(1925)

GENERAL QUIROGA RIDES TO HIS DEATH IN A CARRIAGE

The watercourse dry of puddles, not a drop of water left,
and a moon gone out in the cold shiver of dawn,
and the countryside, poor as a church mouse, dying of hunger.

The coach swayed from side to side, creaking up the slope;
a great bulk of a coach, voluminous, funereal.
Four black horses with a tinge of death in their dark coats
were drawing six souls in terror and one wide awake and bold.

Alongside the postilions a black man was galloping.
To ride to your death in a carriage—what a splendid thing to do!
General Quiroga[1] had in mind to approach the haunts of death
taking six or seven companions with slit throats as escort.

That gang from Córdoba, troublemakers, loudmouthed, shifty
(Quiroga was pondering), now what can they possibly do to me?
Here I am strong, secure, well set up in life
like the stake for tethering beasts to, driven deep in the pampa.

I, who have endured through thousands of afternoons
and whose name alone is enough to set the lances quivering,

---

1 The *gaucho caudillo* Juan Facundo Quiroga, known as the "Jaguar of the Plains," was assassinated in his carriage by agents of the dictatorial governor of the Province of Buenos Aires, Juan Manuel de Rosas, in 1835. [AR]

will not lay down my life in this godforsaken wilderness.
Do the winds from the southwest die, by any chance? Do swords?

But when the brightness of day shone on Barranca Yaco
weapons without mercy swooped in a rage upon him;
death, which is for all, rounded up the man from La Rioja
and more than one thrust of the dagger invoked Juan Manuel de
    Rosas.

Now dead, now on his feet, now immortal, now a ghost,
he reported to the Hell marked out for him by God,
and under his command there marched, broken and bloodless,
the souls in purgatory of his soldiers and his horses.

[1925]   *[AR]*

THE FULL EXTENT OF MY HOPE

(1926)

CARRIEGO AND
THE MEANING OF
THE *ARRABAL*

On a street in the Palermo district of Buenos Aires whose name I most certainly wish to remember, Honduras Street, lived, during the emphatic years of the centennial, a man from Entre Ríos, consumptive, and almost genial, who looked at the neighborhood with an eternalizing gaze. That day-before-yesterday in Palermo was not exactly identical to its today. There were almost no tall buildings, and behind the brick-faced *zaguanes* and the parallel balustrades, the patios abounded in sky, in grape arbors, and girls. There were vacant lots that hosted the sky, and in the afternoons, the moon seemed more alone, and light carrying the strong aroma of *caña* emanated from the back rooms of stores. The neighborhood was for fighters in that day-before-yesterday: People were proud that it was called Tierra del Fuego, and the mythological scarlet of Palermo de San Benito still persisted on the knives of the compadres.

In those days, there were *compadritos*: Foulmouthed men who whiled away their time behind a whistle or a cigarette and whose distinctive traits were a high-combed mane of hair, a silk handkerchief, high-heeled shoes, a bent-over gait, and a challenging gaze. It was the classic time of gangs, of Indians. Bravery or the simulation of bravery was one kind of happiness, and Ño Moreira (a river-edge man from Matanzas elevated by Eduardo Gutiérrez to demigod) was still the Luis Ángel Firpo the local thugs invoked. Evaristo Carriego (the man from Entre Ríos I mentioned at the outset) stared forever at those things and enunciated them in verses that are the soul of our soul.

So much is this the case that *arrabal* and Carriego are synonyms for a single vision. A vision perfected by death and reverence, since the death of the person who caused it surrounds
that vision with piety and ties it to the past with definitive firm-
ness. His modest twenty-nine years and his early death lend
prestige to that pathetic setting, characteristic of his work. They
have invested him with gentleness, which means that in José
Gabriel's fabulization of him, we find an extremely reduced,
almost womanish Carriego who is by no means the great foulmouthed creature and permanent chatterbox I saw on Sundays
on Serrano Street during my childhood.

His poems have been properly judged by all. But what I want
to emphasize is that despite a great deal of notorious and awkward sensitivity, they have facets of tenderness, intelligence, and
perspicacity, as seen in this example:

> And when they aren't there, for
> how long will their darling voices
> echo in the deserted house?
> How will the faces be
> in memory of those we
> shall never see again?

I want to praise completely his prosopopoeia of the barrel
organ, a composition Oyuela considers his best, and which I
judge to be made of perfection:

> Most nights the blind man waits for you
> sitting at the door. He's silent and listens.
> Blurred memories of distant things
> he evokes in silence, of things
> when his eyes had mornings,
> when he was young . . . his girl . . . who knows!

The soul of the stanza above is not in the final line; it's in the
penultimate, and I suspect that Carriego put it there in order
not to be emphatic. In another, earlier composition, "The Soul
of the Suburb," I sketched out the same subject, and it's beauti-

ful to compare his first picture (a realist picture composed of minuscule observations) with the definitive, grave, and tender party, where he convokes the favorite symbols of his art: the seamstress who made that fatal mistake, the moon, the blind man.

All of them sad symbols. They depress the will to live instead of encouraging it. Nowadays it's usual to suppose that a lack of vital will and a cowardly, overly sad lament are the essence of *arrabalero* sentiment. I don't think so. A few stretches of the accordion aren't enough to convince me. Neither are the low-down sufferings of sentimental thugs and more or less repentant prostitutes. The contemporary tango, made totally out of picturesque and worked-over *lunfardo*, is one thing, and quite another the old tangos made of pure insolence, pure shamelessness, pure happiness in bravery. Those were the genuine voice of the *compadrito*: The new ones (music and lyrics) are the fiction of those incredulous about comradeship, those who explain things and create disillusion. The primordial tangos—"The Cabaret," "The Mustang," "The Argentine Apache," "A Night of Fun," and "Hotel Victoria"—testify to the ribald bravery of the *arrabal*. Lyrics and music complement each other. From the tango "Don Juan, the Neighborhood Hit Man," I recall these bad and tough verses:

> When I tango I'm so bodacious
> that when I do a double cut,
> the word spreads through the Northside
> if I happen to be on the Southside.

But they're old, and today we go to the *arrabal* seeking a repertory of failures. It's clear that Evaristo Carriego seems somewhat to blame for this lugubriousness of our vision. He, more than anyone else, has darkened the bright color of the outskirts of Buenos Aires; he is innocently guilty of the fact that in tangos, the sluts go unanimously to the hospital and the compadres are broken down by morphine.

In this sense, his work is antithetical to that of Alvarez, who was from Entre Ríos and who learned how to be a *porteño*.

Even so, we have to confess that Alvarez's vision has little or no lyrical importance, while that of Carriego is enslaving. He's filled our eyes with pity, and we all know that pity needs misery and weakness in order to be sorry for them later. Which is why we have to forgive him the fact that none of the girls in his book ever gets a boyfriend. If he arranged things that way, it was in order to love them better and reveal his heart turned into pity for their sorrow.

This extremely brief note on Carriego has a secret side, and I'm going to go back to it someday, only in order to enhance his image. I suspect that Carriego is in heaven (in some heaven like Palermo, doubtless the same one where the Portones were taken), where the Jew Heinrich Heine will visit him and they're already on friendly terms.

[1926]   [AMA]

THE FULL EXTENT
OF MY HOPE

It's to *criollos* I wish to speak, men who feel that it is in this land where they live and die, not to those who believe the sun and moon are in Europe. This is a land of men born as exiles, of men nostalgic for the distant and the different: They are the real gringos, whether their blood authorizes it or not. With them my pen does not speak.

I wish to speak to the others, to our own boys attached to this earth who do not minimize the reality of this country. My subject today is the fatherland: what there is in it of present, past, and future. And let's be clear: the future never has the nerve to be the present completely without first trying things out, and that trying things out is hope. Blessed be you, hope, memory of the future, scent of that which is to come, God's first stroke of the pen.

What have we Argentines accomplished? The ejection of the English from Buenos Aires was perhaps the first great *criollo* deed. The War of Independence was charged with the romantic grandeur appropriate to those times, but it's hard to count it as a popular enterprise, and it took place at the other end of America. The Holy Federation was the *porteño* "live and let live" turned into a norm, a genuinely *criollo* organism that the *criollo* Urquiza (without really realizing what he was doing) killed at Monte Caseros when he defeated Rosas. It spoke with no other voice but the rancorous and uncouth language of emblems and the posthumous verses of Hernández's *Martín Fierro*.

It was a most beautiful will to *criollismo*, but it never man-aged to think anything, and that stubbornness all its own, that untamed gaucho daydreaming, is less forgivable than its Ma-zorca. Sarmiento (that North-Americanized wild Indian, great hater and misunderstander of everything *criollo*) Europeanized us with his religion of a man newly arrived at culture who ex-pects miracles from it.

After that, what other things have there been here? Lucio V. Mansilla, Estanislao del Campo, and Eduardo Wilde invented more than one perfect page, and in the waning days of the cen-tury, the city of Buenos Aires discovered the tango. Better put, the tango was discovered by the *arrabales*, Saturday nights, girls, the *compadritos* with that bent-over gait of theirs. I still have to take care of the quarter-century that runs from 1900 to 1925, and I sincerely judge that three names, Evaristo Carriego, Macedonio Fernández, and Ricardo Güiraldes, should not be omitted. Fame mentions other names, but I don't believe it. Groussac, Lugones, Ingenieros, Enrique Banchs are people of a period but not of a lineage. They do well what others already did, and that schoolish criterion of well or badly done is just a matter of technique that should not worry us here where we're tracking the elemental, the stuff of origins. Nevertheless, their renown is true, and for that reason I mentioned them.

I've reached the end of my examination (of my generalized and rapid examination), and I think the reader will agree with me if I state that our accomplishments have been essentially poor. These lands have not engendered a mystic or a metaphysi-cian, not one feeler or understander of life! Our greatest man is still don Juan Manuel de Rosas: exemplar of the strength of the individual, great certainty of knowing oneself alive, but inca-pable of erecting something spiritual, and tyrannized ultimately more than anyone else by his own tyranny and bureaucracy.

With regard to General San Martín, he's just a general made of mist for us, wearing epaulets and decorations of mist. Among the men who walk the streets of my Buenos Aires, there is only one privileged by legend, and he passes like a closed car: That man is Irigoyen. And among the dead? Much has been written on the extremely distant Santos Vega, but he is just an empty name that passes from pen to pen without substantial content. So for Ascasubi he was a chattering old man, and for Rafael Obligado he was a country man made of nobility, and for Eduardo Gutiérrez he was a hyperbolically romantic outlaw, an idyllic precursor of Moreira. His legend is no such thing. There are no legends in this land, and not a single ghost walks our streets. That is our dishonor.

Our vital reality is grandiose and our thought reality is impoverished. No idea has been engendered here that resembles my Buenos Aires, my innumerable Buenos Aires, which is a tenderness of trees in Belgrano and long sweetness in Almagro, and reluctant *orillero* sarcasm in Palermo, and much sky in Villa Ortúzar, and taciturn eminences in Cinco Esquinas, and the favorite spot of sunsets in Villa Urquiza, and a ring of pampa in Saavedra.

"Yet America is a poem in our eyes; its ample geography dazzles the imagination, and it will not wait long for metres," wrote Emerson in 1844 ("The Poet") in a declaration that sounds like a prefiguration of Whitman and that today in the Buenos Aires of 1925 is once again prophetic. More than a city, Buenos Aires is a country, and we must find for it the poetry, the music, the painting, the religion, and the metaphysics appropriate to its grandeur. This is the full extent of my hope, which invites all of us to be gods and to work toward its incarnation.

I want neither progressivism nor *criollismo* in the way those words are commonly used. The first means subjecting ourselves to being almost-North-Americans or almost-Europeans, a tenacious being almost-others. The second, once a word of action (the horseman's mockery of pedestrians, the mockery of those born on horseback toward those born on their feet), is today a word of nostalgia (the slack appetite for the countryside, the illusion of feeling oneself a bit like Moreira). Not much fervor in either, and I'm sorry about that with regard to *criollismo*. It's true that widening the meaning of that word—today it usually means a mere *gauchismo*—might be the task that has the most affinities with my project. *Criollismo* by all means, but a *criollismo* that converses with the world and with the individual and with God and with death. Let's see if someone helps me find it.

Our famous skepticism doesn't discourage me. Disbelief, if it is intense, is also faith and can be the wellspring of works. We see it in Lucian and Swift and Laurence Sterne and George Bernard Shaw. A grandiose, vehement disbelief can be our great accomplishment.

[1926]   [AMA]

THE PAMPA AND THE
SUBURBIO ARE GODS

The *arrabal* and the pampa: two presences of God, two realities that arouse our reverence so powerfully that the mere enunciation of their names is sufficient to add grandeur to any verse and raise our hearts with moving and harsh jubilation. Both already have their legend, and I wish I could write them with capital letters, the better to show their true nature: They are archetypal things, not subject to the contingencies of time. Even so, mentioning God may seem a bit exaggerated to some, so I'd be better off defining them with the word *totem*, in the most widely accepted sense of that term, as things consubstantial with a race or an individual. (*Totem* is an Algonquin word: English researchers disseminated it, and it figures in the works of Spengler and F. Graebner—works translated by Ortega y Gasset in his Germanization of Hispanic thought.)

Pampa. Who found the word *pampa*, that infinite word that is like a sound and its echo? All I know is that it is of Quechuan origin, that its primitive meaning is "that of plain" and that it seems to be spoken syllable by syllable by the *pampero*, the fierce wind of the pampa. Colonel Hilario Ascasubi, in his notes to *Los mellizos de la Flor* [The Twins from La Flor Ranch], writes that the gauchos took pampa to mean the open land on the other side of the frontier traveled by Indian tribes. Even then, the word *pampa* was a word for the far away. We should make use of the colonel not only for that fact but so we remember some verses of his. Here are a few:

> Thus the pampa and the outland
> at the hour of midday
> seemed a waste,
> since from one horizon to the other
> there was not one little bird to be seen.

And here are some more:

> The whole pampa gave birth to
> flowers of soft fragrance,
> at the same time that an enchanting glow
> crowned the mountains in the distance.

That expression made of two total words, *whole pampa*, is agreeable next to the part about the flowers, because it's as if we were seeing simultaneously a great power and a great calm, an infinite power revealing itself in gifts. But what I really wish to show is that in both quotations, the pampa is defined by its greatness. Does that greatness really exist? Darwin rejects the idea totally and rationalizes his incredulity in this way: "On the high sea, with a person's eyes six feet above the level of the water, his horizon is two and four-fifths miles away. In the same way, the flatter a plain is, the more the horizon approaches these narrow limits: something, to my way of thinking, that entirely nullifies the greatness one imagines beforehand for a great plain."

William Henry Hudson, very much a *criollo* though an Englishman, born and raised in our province, transcribes and ratifies Darwin's observation (*The Naturalist in the Plata*, 1892).

So why doubt it? Why not accept the fact that our empirical knowledge of the spaciousness of the pampa tricks our eyes and augments it with its memories? I myself, disbelieving myself, as I write out these doubts in a house in the Recoleta neighborhood, went, a few days ago, to Saavedra, at about number 5000 on Cabildo and saw the first little farms and some *ombú* trees, and again the earth became round, and the countryside looked enormous to me. It's true I went there in a reverential mood, and, like so many Argentines, I'm the grandson and even great-grandson of ranchers. In a land of shepherds like this one, it's natural that we think of open country with emotion, natural that its most lasting symbol—the pampa—should be revered by all.

To the complete pampa symbol, whose human incarnation is the gaucho, we add over time that of the riverbanks: a symbol in the making. Rafael Cansinos Assens (*Literary Themes and Their Interpretation*, p. 24 et seq.) says that the *arrabal* lyrically represents an undetermined effusion and sees it as strange and combative. That is one face of the truth. In this Buenos Aires of mine, the Babelic, the picturesque, the detached from the four corners of the earth, is the decorous nature of the Centro. The Moorish center is in Reconquista, and the Jewish center in Talcahuano and Libertad. Entre Ríos, Callao, Avenida de Mayo are vehemence; Núñez and Villa Alvear the chores and daydreams of the *maté* drinker's idle hours, the very *criollo* siesta in the *zaguán*, and prolonged games of *truco*. Those old-time tangos, excessive and so soft on their hard spine of virility: "Cargo," "North Wind," "The Cabaret" are the perfect sound of that soul.

Nothing in literature equals them. Fray Mocho and his follower Félix Lima are the chatty layabouts of the *arrabal*; Evaristo Carriego, the sadness of its disillusion, its failure. Then I came along (as long as I'm alive I won't lack for someone to praise me), and I spoke, before anyone else, not about destinies, but about the landscape of the outskirts: the shop pink as a cloud, the alleys. Roberto Arlt and José S. Tallon are the insolence of the *arrabal*, its bravura.

Each one of us has pronounced his little shred of the suburb: No one has said all there is to say. I forgot Marcelo del Mazo, who in the second series of *The Conquered* (Buenos Aires, 1910) possesses some admirable pages, unjustly overlooked. With regard to the *History of the Arrabal* by Manuel Gálvez, it paraphrases the lyrics from any tango, very proseified and broken down. (I most certainly do not have such a bad opinion of all tango lyrics and like some a great deal. For instance, that most ineffable parody of "The Apache" and "The Silver Bell" by Linnig, with its Quevedoisms like "over the light from the streetlamp that bleeds onto the knife," and that passionate girl cut on the mouth who says to the thug, "Your dagger made my kisses bigger.")

There can be no doubt that the *arrabal* and the pampa both exist completely, and that I feel them open like wounds that pain me equally.

We're all on our own here, our hearts confirm no faith, but we do believe in four things: the pampa is a shrine, the first country-man is a real man, the strength of the bad guys, the generous sweetness of the *arrabal*. I am pointing out here not lost lights but four cardinal points. The *Martín Fierro*, the *Santos Vega*, the other *Santos Vega*, the *Facundo* all look toward the first things I said the lasting works of this twentieth century will look toward the final things.

With regard to mountains or the sea, no *criollo* living any-where near the river has known how to see them, and our po-etry may stand as an example of that. The sunny spot of sea in the *Fausto* is not intensity, it is spectacle: It's a glance from shore, it's light and glitters like the dew on the leaves. Of the indefatigable wealth of the world, only the *arrabal* and the pampa belong to us. Ricardo Güiraldes, the brightest star in our letters, prays to the plain; I—if God is kind—shall sing to the *arrabal* for a third time, in a better voice, better advised by grace than before. Something, as one who wasn't a *criollo* (Ben Jonson, *The Poetaster*) said:

> That must and shall be sung high and aloof,
> Safe from the wolf's black jaw and the dull ass's hoof.

[1926]   [AMA]

THE PURPLE LAND

The Germans (when they actually do understand) are grandiose connoiseurs who elevate everything to the level of symbol and fearlessly categorize the world. They understand people, but only *sub specie aeternitatis* and by pigeonholing them in an order. The Spaniards believe in the ill will of others and in their own grammar, but not that there are other countries. The French too do not understand the totality, and all geography (physical or political, let it be understood—let's not even speak of spiritual geography) is an error in the face of their pride.

On the other hand, the English—at least the migratory and wandering English—possess a faculty for soaking up foreign variations of being, a slow, instinctive disanglicization that Americanizes, Asiatizes, Africanizes, and redeems them. Goethe, Hegel, and Spengler have elevated the world into symbols, but a greater feat is that of Browning, who dressed himself in dozens of souls (some vile, like Caliban, others absurd) and versified for them a series of impassioned allegations, justifying them before God. To anyone who asks me for more examples, I shall recall the life of the Japanized Lafcadio Hearn and of Captain Richard Burton, who made the pilgrimage to Mecca without the Muslims (who accompanied him to the Kaaba) noticing anything in him that was improper in a Muslim. There was as well George Borrow, the gypsy Englishman who spoke *caló* as well as any *chalán* from Córdoba, and this great Hudson, an Englishman who hailed from Chascomús in the Province of Buenos Aires. He was a man of universal knowledge, who smack in the heart of the nineteenth century, during progressism at full cry and afterism, exalted *criollez*. He did it in *The Purple Land*, a sequence of fighting adventures and love adventures.

It is about this primordial novel of *criollismo* that I wish to speak to you: a book more ours than sorrow, only distanced from us by the English language, from which one day it will have to be restored to the pure *criollo* in which it was thought—*criollo* of the outskirts, *criollo* in goodness and in scorn, *criollo* of the widest time never ticked at by watches and measured slowly by *matés*.

It has barely any plot. A certain Richard Lamb—recently married to an Argentine girl who stays behind in Montevideo—travels the Uruguayan countryside inch by inch and gets involved with many lives and a couple of hearts. This Lamb is a great boy: clever, a redresser of crimes, a lover (that's what Cervantes calls those who fall in love easily and hard), and apt for all nobility, be it of thought or passion. He also has opinions: the opinions of others, which he can shed, about the advantageousness of culture, mere additions that fall off after a few months of wandering from ranch to ranch and which he rejects with pathetic violence.

The penultimate chapter—where Lamb from the bald Sinai of the Cerro blesses gaucho life and pronounces an apology for instinct and the condemnation of laws—is the rational summary of the work. There, clearly and finally, is the dilemma exacerbated by Sarmiento in his bawling civilization and barbarism, a dilemma Hudson/Lamb resolves unhesitatingly by opting for barbarism. That is, he opts for naturalness, for impulse, for the untied, unfriendly life without stretching or formulas. That and nothing else is the famous barbarism. The thugs of Rosas's Mazorca were never the only incarnation of *criollez*.

Hudson, through the mouth of Lucero—a Flores horse-breaker and a great *pulpería* conversationalist, who chats in his novel—can't abide politics and says of it that it is nothing more than an urban intromission into rural life. Spengler said the same thing to me a couple of nights ago on page 113 of his second, still-untranslated volume . . . Hudson's *criollo* sentiment, made up of unbroken independence, of a stoic acceptance of suffering, and of a serene acceptance of good fortune, resembles that of José Hernández. But Hernández, a great member of the Federal Party who fought under the orders of don Prudencio Rozas, the disillusioned ex-Federal who found out about Caseros and the failure of gauchoism in Urquiza, did not die within his faith. Martín Fierro himself belied it with this most unfortunate palinode that appears at the end of his work, where we find declarations of this cast: "The gaucho should have a house—School, Church, and rights." All of which is pure Sarmientoism.

Another difference that stands between the *Martín Fierro* and *The Purple Land* is the irremediable difference between a tragic destiny—the inevitability of suffering—and a happy destiny, which despite hatreds and delays, never banishes its certitude of love. This is the great dissimilarity between Lamb's fervent twenty-five years and Fierro's forty sententious years.

The Purple Land was written by someone curious about lives, one who took pleasure in the many varieties of the ego. Hudson never gets angry with the narrators of his tale, never berates them, shouts at them, or doubts the democratic truth that the other is also an ego and that "I" for that person may be an "if only he weren't." Hudson elevates and justifies what cannot be substituted in each soul he delves into: its virtues, its defects, even its particular way of making mistakes.

This means he's drawn some unforgettable destinies: those of the outlaw Santa Coloma; of Candelaria; of the English immigrants, who make a big point of their obligatory energy while being very broken down by rum; also the destinies of the miserable Epifanio Claro; and the saddest and most beautiful of all: Mónica, the peasant girl of the Yí who gives all her love to an outsider, gives it simply, as one might give a glance.

These lives and those that pass through the list of stories that make up *El Ombú* are not eternal archetypes; they are as episodic and real as those invented by God. To experience them is to add bright lives—almost always noble as well—to one's own and expand it into a crowd. Richard Lamb is eternal. He is the hero of all fables, the extremely normal Quixote who only needs to be hopeful and daring, in the way women only need to be good and pretty. Listening to him live, I've envied him with some frequency without ever losing my friendship for him. How much country moon for a single man, how many fights with no fear and an alert heart, how much casual love to be remembered later in the security of one's only love!

[1925]   *[AMA]*

LEOPOLDO LUGONES: *ROMANCERO*

In this book, don Leopoldo Lugones proves himself to be almost no one, very clumsy, very free with the stuffing. The last item, however, is the least important. What does it matter whether the poetic line be well or badly made? The best Castilian sonnets that have aroused my fervor, those my lips have carried in solitude (the one by Enrique Banchs to the mirror, Juan Ramón Jiménez's "Fleeting Return," and that extremely painful sonnet by Lope de Vega about Jesus spending winter nights waiting for Lope in vain) also contain padding.

The Parnassians (bad carpenters and jewelers trying to be poets) talk about perfect sonnets, but I've never seen one anywhere. Besides, what is all this about perfection? A circle is a perfect form, and soon after we look at it, it bores us. It's also possible to assert that with Lugones's system, padding is inevitable. If a poet rhymes in Spanish with words that end in *ía* or *aba*, there are hundreds of words available to finish off a stanza, and the stuffing therefore is shameful stuffing. On the other hand, if he rhymes using a word ending in *ul,* as Lugones does, he has to *azular* (to blue) something right away and then arrange a trip so he can carry a *baúl* (suitcase) or other indignities. In the same way, someone who rhymes using *arde* commits himself to this ridiculous obligation: *I don't know what I'll say to you, but I commit myself to think awhile about the "brasero" (because it burns—"arde") and another while about five-thirty (afternoon, "tarde"), and yet another while about bragging*

(alarde), and still another about some *yellowbelly (coward,*
"cobarde").

The classics felt that way, and if they ever rhymed *baúl* with
azul, or *calostro* (colostrum) with *rostro* (face), it was in joking
compositions where those rhymes are appropriate. Lugones
does it seriously. Let's see, friends, what do you think of this
little gem?

> Illusion that its wings doth spread *(tiende)*
> In a fragile bow of tulle *(tul)*
> And in the sensitive heart doth stick *(prende)*
> Its insidious pin so blue *(azul)*

This quatrain is the last card in the deck, and it's terrible, not
only because of the miserable rhymes it bears but because of its
spiritual misery, because of the insignificance of its soul. This
say-nothing quatrain, silly and frivolous, sums up the *Romanc-*
ero. The sin of this book resides in its nonexistence, in its being
almost a book of blank pages annoyingly dotted with lilies, rib-
bons, silks, roses, fountains, and other colorful consequences of
gardening and tailoring. Of dressmaking in point of fact.

I've pointed out that Rosaleda de Castro, with her swans and
pavilions, was the only disciple of Rubén Darío alive in Buenos
Aires. Today I admit I was wrong. The tribe of Rubén is still
alive and kicking, like a full moon reflected in a pool, and this
Romancero proves it. An irreparable and painful proof.

I read it with goodwill, and I can declare that except for the
first and last *kasida* and some of the *Lieder*, there is nothing in
it that is not a new edition of the immemorial errors of Poetry,
of those crevices through which death appears. Lugones doesn't
understand the most elementary and clear things, and he even
has to gold-plate the sun and turn the singing of the birds into
pearls. He says of a poor nocturnal frog that it is "a crystal key
on the moon's piano." Metaphors that ennoble make me happy,
but not these, which reduce everything to junk.

The *Romancero* is very much a book of its author. Don Leopoldo has forgotten books because he's given himself over to
exercises of ventriloquism, and it may be said that no intellec-

tual labor is alien to him except that of invention. (Not a single idea here is his own; there is not a single landscape in the universe that belongs to him by right of conquest. He has looked on nothing with the eyes of eternity.) Today, so close to glory and resting from the tenacious exercise of being a permanent genius, he's wanted to speak in his own voice, and we've heard it in the *Romancero*, and he has expressed his nothingness. How shameful for his admirers, what a humiliation!

[1926]   [AMA]

FROM

THE LANGUAGE OF
THE ARGENTINES

(1928)

TRUCO

Forty cards seek to displace life. In the players' hands, the new deck creaks or the old one sticks: cardboard nothings that come to life, an ace of spades that will be as omnipotent as don Juan Manuel de Rosas, potbellied little horses Velázquez copied. The dealer shuffles those little pictures. The thing is easy to say and even to do, but the magical and outrageous aspect of the game—of the act of playing—sprouts in the action. Forty is the number of cards, and 1 by 2 by 3 by 4 . . . by 40 the ways they can come out. It's a number delicately exact in its enormity, with an immediate predecessor and unique successor, but it's not foretold. It's a remote cipher of vertigo that seems to dissolve in its mob those who play.

Thus, from the start, the central mystery of the game is adorned with another mystery: that there are numbers. On the table, the cloth removed so the cards can slide, await the chickpeas in their pile, also arithmetized. The *truco* match is ready to start: The players, suddenly criollized, shed their usual identity. A different "I," an almost ancestral and vernacular "I," captures the projects of the game. Suddenly the language is other. Tyrannical prohibitions, astute possibilities and impossibilities weigh over every utterance. To say *flor* without having three cards in one suit is a criminal and punishable act, but if you've already said *envido* (bet), it doesn't matter. To mention one of the *lances* (hands) in *truco* means committing oneself to it, an obligation that continues folding itself into euphemisms with each play. *Quiebro* (I break) means *quiero* (I want, or I'll take that bet); *envite* (you bet) means *envido* (I bet); an *olorosa* (fragrant) or *jardinera* (garden girl) means *flor* (flower). It's proper that in the mouths of those who lose there echoes this pronouncement of the kind a local gang leader would utter: *A ley de juego, todo está dicho: falta envido y truco, y si hay flor ¡contraflor al resto!* [All's fair in cards within the rules: All we need is betting and winning tricks, and if you say *flor* I'll double that!] The dialogue works itself up to the point of poetry more than once. *Truco* contains recipes for hanging on for losers; verses also for exaltation.

Truco is as memorable as a calendar date. Fireside and barroom *milongas*, funeral jokes, bullying in the style of Roca and Tejedor, insolence straight from the houses of Junín and from their stepmother in Temple: This is the human commerce it nurtures. *Truco* is a good singer, especially when it's winning or pretending to win: It sings at intersections at nightfall, from taverns with some light in them.

The usual thing in *truco* is lying. The style of its trickery is not that of poker: mere discouraging or seeking to depress an opponent into doubts and to put at risk a pile of chips during one hand or another. Lying in *truco* is the action of a lying voice, of a face judged face to face and that defends itself, of tricky and crazy chatter. An empowering of fraud takes place in *truco*: The complaining player who tosses his cards on the table may well be hiding a good hand (elementary astuteness). This *criollo* game is comfortable in time and chatty, but its savor derives from mischief. It's the placing of mask upon mask, and its spirit is that of the trinket sellers Moishe and Daniel who greet each other on the great plain of Russia:

"Where are you going, Daniel?"

"To Sevastapol," he says.

Then Moishe looked him up and down and declared:

"You're lying, Daniel. You tell me you're going to Sevastapol so I'll think you're going to Nijni-Novgorod, but the truth is you are going to Sevastapol. You're lying, Daniel!"

I consider the *truco* players. It's as if they are hidden in the *criollo* noise of dialogue. They want to frighten life away by shouting. Forty cards—amulets of painted cardboard, cheap mythology, exorcisms—are enough for them to conjure away common living. They play with their backs to the trafficked hours of the world. Public and urgent reality, where we all are, is just outside their gathering but doesn't enter. The space of their table is another country. It's populated by "I'll bet" and "I'll take that bet," the criss-crossed *flor* and the unexpected nature of its gift, the avid adventure novel of each hand, the 7 of *oros* jingling hope and other impassioned bagatelles of the repertory. The *truco* players live in that hallucinated little world. They foment it with bad and dirty jokes that take their time; they tend it as if it were a fire. It is, I know, a narrow world: the ghost of local politics and sins, a world after all invented by corral-bred wizards and neighborhood warlocks, but for all that, no less able to replace this real world, which is diabolical and less inventive in its ambition.

To think about a local story like this one about *truco* and not leave it or not deepen it—the two figures may here symbolize the same act, their precision is so great—seems to me a very serious futility. I want not to forget here a thought about the poverty of *truco*. The diverse levels of its polemics, its twists, its heartbreaks, its cabals, cannot fail to return. Along with experiences, they have to repeat themselves. What is *truco* for someone used to playing it but a custom? Just look at how given to memory the game is; consider its predilection for traditional formulas.

Each player in truth does nothing more than take part in remote hands, that is, periods of past lives. Generations of *criollos*—now invisible—are, as it were, buried alive in *truco*: They are *truco*. That we can assert without metaphors. Thus, by means of such a thought we see that time is a fiction. Thus, by means of those painted-cardboard labyrinths we approach metaphysics: the only justification and finality for all subjects.

[AMA]

TRUCO [1]

Forty cards have taken the place of life.
The decorated cardboard talismans
make us oblivious of our destiny,
and a light-hearted game
goes on filling up our stolen time
with the flowery flourishes
of a home made mythology.
Within the limits of the table
the life of others comes to a standstill.
Inside the game is an alien country,
the ups and downs of bidding and accepting,
the domination of the ace of spades,
omnipotent, like don Juan Manuel, [2]
and the seven of diamonds, a jingling of hope.
A furtive slowing-down
keeps all words in check,
and, as the vagaries of the game
repeat and repeat themselves,
the players of that evening
reenact ancient tricks:

1 "Truco" first appeared in *Fervor de Buenos Aires* (1923), but it makes sense to place it here in the section *The Language of the Argentines*, next to the essay of the same name. [AMA]

2 The Argentine dictator Juan Manuel de Rosas (1793–1877). [AR]

An act that brings to life, but very faintly,
the generations of our forefathers
who bequeathed to the leisure time of Buenos Aires
truco, with all its bids and its deceptions.

[1923] *[AR]*

GENEALOGY OF
THE TANGO

The tango is the most widely known Argentine accomplishment. The one that has insolently made Argentina famous everywhere on earth. Obviously, we should investigate its origins and construct for it a genealogy that will lack neither deifying legends nor ascertainable truths. The matter was discussed in detail back in 1913, but now don Vicente Rossi's book, *Cosas de negros* [Black Matters] (Córdoba, 1926), has again brought it to our attention. I've written elsewhere [in the magazine *Valoraciones*, 1926] about Rossi's book, about the continuous pleasure its reading imparts and its inevitable factual errors. Today I want to restate his thesis and amplify it.

Rossi's theory is circumstantial: The so-called Argentine tango is the child of the Montevidean *milonga* and grandchild to the *habanera*. It was born in the Academia San Felipe, a Montevidean warehouse used for public dances attended by *compadritos* and blacks. It emigrated to the Buenos Aires Bajo, where it pushed and shoved its way through the Cuartos de Palermo (where it was received by blacks and camp followers). It made a racket in the houses of ill repute of the Centro and in Monserrat until the Teatro Nacional exalted it.

That is, the tango is Afro-Montevidean, the tango has black blood. To be nonwhite and Uruguayan are *criollo* conditions, but Argentine blacks (and even those who aren't black) are as *criollo* as those across the river, and there is no reason to suppose that everything was invented over there. Someone will say that there is the effective reason that it happened that way, but such chicanery will not satisfy our engorged patriotism. In fact, it stirs it up even more and pushes it to despair.

Perhaps we should recall here the analogous case of the origins of Christopher Columbus. To claim him for their own, the Italians must cling to the simple fact of his birth certificate or to local anecdote, i.e., that the admiral was born in Genoa and was 100 percent Italian. The Spaniards have a better argument. They can say that since the discovery of America and its conquest were manifestly Spanish enterprises, there is no historical reason to introduce the Genoese into the business. (Besides, what Genoese could there be when their home in La Boca del Riachuelo was yet to be discovered?) It's a shame they didn't dare to be frank and chose instead falsification, mythology, and gossip over faith. I'll be more sincere than they and will resolutely declare that the tango is *porteño*. The people of Buenos Aires recognize themselves in it fully, which is not the case of the people of Montevideo, always nostalgic for gauchos. In any case, I'm more convinced of the Uruguayan origin of Rossi than of the Uruguayan origin of the tango.

All pragmatism aside, don Vicente Rossi's thesis may be honorably reduced to this syllogism:

The *milonga* belongs exclusively to Montevideo.
The *milonga* is the origin of the tango.
The origin of the tango is Montevidean.

I accept the fact that the minor premise is unshakable. On the other hand, I have no faith in the major premise and know of no valid argument to back it up. Rossi limits himself to writing: "In Argentina, the *milonga* was not used as song, nor was the dance called the *milonga* danced." He then sends us to a note published in *La Nación* in 1887, where we see that the word *milonga* does not appear in any *lunfardo* dialogue. As we see, his argument is negative and unconvincing. Inversely, who doesn't remember a certain ineffable (ineffable in its obscenity) *milonga* written about Carlos Tejedor, a *milonga* whose outrageously insulting eloquence authorizes us to suppose it contemporaneous with the fact it names, that is, to date it back to 1880? It begins like this:

Don Carlos de Tejedor
with a mad patience

and it's still a way to brag when you get a winning hand in *truco*. Also, don Rodolfo Senet (Buenos Aires, ca. 1880, *La Prensa*, October 17, 1926) talks about the *milongas* that celebrated the first trolleys and the first paved streets on the outskirts of town. One of the latter advises:

Be careful with the paving stones
you're really gonna fall,
and a blow from those hard paving stones
will really make you bawl.

Oh *compadritos* from Ombú Street and from Europa Street, what *capitis diminutio*, what vacillation for your vertiginous high-heeled dignity the pointy paving stones must have been, so Andean, so foreign, so untypical to the Creole dirt of the thoroughfare.

Up until now, I've given free rein to my conjectures. Now we'll let the facts do the talking. Ventura R. Lynch's *Cancionero bonaerense* [Buenos Aires Songbook]—a book published in 1883!—studies the *milonga*, declares it to be widespread among the cheap dance halls in the suburbs as well as the casinos in Plaza del Once and Plaza de Constitución. He says it was invented by the *compadritos* to make fun of the *candombero* dancers and even notes that it was played on barrel organs.

Don Miguel A. Camino, a poet, traces another tango genealogy in his beautiful memoir *El tango*. "Chaquiras" appears almost at the end of the book and begins like this:

It was born in the old Corrales
about the year 1880.
The child of a *milonga*
and a hard man from the *arrabal*.
Its godfather was the bugler
of the foreman of the trolley,
and it was in knife fights

> where it was taught to dance.
> Thus it was in the *ocho*,
> and in the *asentada*,
> *la media luna*
> and *el paso atrás*,
> it yielded the reflection
> of the slash
> and the *cuerpeadas*
> of one who plays it out
> with his dagger.

The origin made into verse by Camino is as original as it could possibly be. To the erotic or prostitutional motivation we've all recognized in the tango he adds a bellicose motivation of joyous fighting, of mock combat. I have no idea if that motivation is factually true: what I do know is that it concurs marvelously with old tangos "made of pure nerve, of pure shamelessness, of the pure happiness of courage" as I described them in other pages a year ago. Rossi, who for reasons of chronology is unfamiliar with Camino's explanation, supports it a bit in this paragraph on the *milonga*:

> At that time *milongas* had titles, and they give more proof that the *milonga* was not sensual: Bitter Maté, Bare Faced, Narrow Pass, The Canary, *Kyrie Eleison*, Smelt with Potatoes, Mr. Policeman, etc. They aren't even amorous, because in the brutal Bajo there was no room for idylls. The thugs took advantage of opportunities for sensual activity with the self-satisfaction and lack of concern of men who don't need them, just for real sport. (*Cosas de negros—La academia*.)

It's only right to note that the literati, whenever they've dealt with the tango, have always made much of its melancholy lubricity, its complicated and almost inflamed sensuality. Two strong examples should be enough: that of Marcelo del Mazo, in the second series of *Los vencidos* (1910): "Now then girl, howled the *compadre*, and the sullen partner / offered the shamelessness of her hot immodesty / beating with her flesh,

like a tongue of fire, the vibrating guts of that mob of love";
and that of Ricardo Güiraldes, whose "Tango" (*El cencerro de
cristal* [The Glass Bell], 1915) imposes on us these decisive
lines—"Red stain that coagulates in black. Fatal tango, proud
and crude. Lazily drawn-out notes in a nasal key . . ." Inversely,
the only time Evaristo Carriego bothered to recall the tango
was to see happiness in it, to show its streetlike and festive nature, as it was twenty years ago:

> Out on the street, the good folks pour out
> their most licentious and delinquent remarks
> because to the rhythm of a tango, "La Morocha,"
> two thugs show off elegant twirls.

The two versions of the tango—the merely licentious and the
mischievous—could correspond to two different eras: the first
to this regrettable contemporary episode of low-life elegies in a
studiously *lunfardo* dialect, complete with *bandoneones*; the
other to the good-old (terrible) times of cuts, of electorial stab-
bings, of corners tricked out in bellicose gangs.

(The tango was, in the first place, a plan for dancing, an
indication of where to make the cuts and the flourishes, an actuality without concern, while the contemporary—which is to
say the really old one—already cultivates memories. An adult
awareness of time weighs over it. Just compare "The Little
Bull"or "The Maldonado River" with any of today's tangos.)

Camino explains the tango for us and also points out the
exact place where it was born: the old Corrals. The precision is
tricky. The mock fighting was never limited to Corrales, since
the knife wasn't exclusively the weapon of butchers: It was, in
any neighborhood, the arm of the *compadrito*. Every neighborhood suffered its knife-fighters, always attached to some political committee in some back room. Some enjoyed lasting but
limited fame: Shorty Flores in la Recoleta, The Turk in Batería,
El Noy in the Food Market. They were demigods wearing high-
crowned hats: men of well-practiced skill in knife business who
would challenge one another out of jealousy. The insolence-
charged *milongas* are probably from those times and, clearly,

they originate in the little dance halls and bars. In them we see
the singer refer to his neighborhood in order to challenge
another:

> I'm from the Alto neighborhood,
> I'm from the Retiro neighborhood,
> I'm the guy who doesn't look
> at whoever it is I'm supposed to fight
> and when I'm dancing a *milonga*
> no one ever gets near me.

or:

> Out of the way, I beg of you,
> 'Cause I'm from Tierra 'el Juego.

I think (clearly, my opinion is not obligatory, and I don't want
to inflict it on anyone) the tango may have originated in any
place in the city, be it in the Recoleta Festivals, it doesn't matter
(although it was there, in about 1880, according to Dr. José
Antonio Wilde, that they would usually end with blood on their
blades), or in the melees in Plaza del Once or Constitución—
anywhere but Corrales. My argument is simple: the tango is
manifestly urban or suburban, *porteño*, and Corrales was always an intrusion of the pampa, a true presence of gauchoism
or a neighborly coquetting with being gauchos, very reverent
toward the past and very alien to all invention.

The tango is not countrified: It's *porteño*. Its homeland is the
pink corners of the *suburbio*, not the country; its setting, the
Bajo; its symbol, the weeping willow of the riverbanks, never
the *ombú*.

[1927]   [AMA]

SITUATING ALMAFUERTE

With regard to Almafuerte, the younger generation, almost all of us, are either penitents or apostates. Today we've set him aside; yesterday we were neighbors of his complaints, parishioners of his rage. We don't know what to think of him, and we lack the means to reconcile today's distancing with a by now worn-out veneration.

Those who define Almafuerte don't help us. The panegyrists repeat the enthusiastic sin of Juan Más y Pi, who in 1905 called Almafuerte "master of today's youth"—a "master" imbued with despair and hatred. His detractors, even more mistaken, censure his bad taste, his gigantism, his purple patches, his lack of civility. Both extremes are irrelevant: Almafuerte should not be providing us with lessons on how to live, and he would certainly not allow us to give him lessons in rhetoric. Let's accept his human spectacle, his idiosyncrasies, as just one more aspect of the indefatigable richness of the world. I don't know if we'll ever give him our intimacy, but we will definitely yield to him our admiration.

But first we have to resolve a not-very-hard-fought dispute: the one concerning the dominion that his grandfather Federico—I mean Nietzsche—held over his amoral and melancholy American grandson. Ricardo Rojas, in referring to the words Almafuerte prefixes with "super," speaks of his *vulgar, Nietzschean stutter*; Oyuela writes in an ill-humored way that *The Missionary* is "a terrible rhapsody by Nietzsche, with the superman and all the rest tossed in." Juan Más y Pi talks in terms of coincidences, and at first sight his courtesy does not seem unjustified. Why deny a *criollo* schoolteacher the ability to think the same things that a

German professor of Greek thought before he did? Why suppose that the jaguar is a plagiarism of the tiger, that the *maté* from Misiones is a copy of tea, that the pampa copies the steppes of the Don, and that Pedro Bonifacio Palacios is a copy of Friedrich Wilhelm Nietzsche?

A simple argument invalidates the defense. It's legitimate to accept that Almafuerte, deriving from the same order of ideas as the German (that is, from evolutionary thinking), reached the same conclusions about the senility of Christian morality and the need for the superman, but it is inadmissible that his terminology or symbology also be the same. Unfortunately, many of Almafuerte's utterances belong to the Nietzschean dialect:

> I know that in the long, very long way of the cross,
> that the supersane walk in their dementia . . .

He says that in the *Confiteor Deo*, after a reference (traitorous or challenging, I don't know which) to Nietzsche himself:

> I know that a thousand woodworms have been gnawing
> the most balanced, genial heads:
> the madhouse is filled with crazy Nietzsches
> and the outskirts of town with bohemian Christs.

We all have a clue-tracing urge, but mine has been frustrated because among the no fewer than seven epigraphs that precede "The Missionary," not one comes from *Zarathustra*. Today that seems fine to me. What good does it do to validate in erudite books that final bit of advice, given man to man, given from one human imbalance to another human imbalance? What good does it do to authorize with libraries what we say and don't say with sunsets, desperation, escapes, and God? The very gravity of prophecy requires that causality in eternal deeds. Alone, without mediators, Moses reaches Horeb (famous for its pastures) and speaks with the voice of the Lord in the burning bush. He's chosen by that voice, and he comes down, bedazzled, among the sheep, transformed into the savior of his people. Almafuerte too, from his tenement and his pampa, wants to listen directly to God.

He profoundly believed in the need to be good and in the bizarre uselessness of ethics, and these two articles of faith survived the aimless wandering of his discourse. He was a great hater of philanthropists, theologians, moralists; he never tolerated forgiveness (for what it contains of condescension, of some domestic Last Judgment exercised by one man over another) and understood that the only nonhumiliating mercy would be that of becoming as dark as the blind man, as marginalized as a cripple, and as tearful as someone sad.

Almafuerte wanted, literally, to *sym-pathize*, that is to suffer with others. He became a mad preacher of goodness, and his blessings were as lacerating as a curse. His cross was the cross of the sword's hilt. Right and left, with a double edge and a point, he wielded his incorruptible and hard virtue. He was certainly odious and possibly genial. He was a speechmaker like no other; nowadays we are reluctant to judge those who speak out a lot. He was the father of almost infinite metaphors, in no way inferior, in their ability to dazzle, to those of any other:

> What your kisses might be in colliding
> if two mobs of kisses collide

is what he vociferates in *The Immortal*.

I've intentionally showcased these two verses. They are an abbreviation or cipher of Almafuerte's modus operandi and nicely embody his expression: originality, pedagogic grumbling, gigantism, banality, robustness. Crudity and banality in the same soul? It is on that duality of Palacios that his critics have tripped themselves up and continue to do so without seeing that both qualities can coexist and that their cohabitation is proverbial in a certain kind of *criollo*.

I'm speaking about the *compadrito* who is (or was) the confluence of many emphases: roughness, emphatic simulation of vigor, banality, emphatic simulation of eloquence; the cult of the murderer, emphasis on courage. The challenges tossed out by a *compadrito* are more daring than a cart driver's aggressiveness: It's the carnation behind one ear, the clever glimpses of the gestures and songs a winning *truco* hand can flourish. The suburb is sewer water and alleys, but it's also the handrail with the tint of a girl and the garden in the patio and the cage with its canary. That's how Carriego understood it, and that duality of mud and elegance was his most felicitous realization:

> With regard to the girls, what airs they put on!,
> as if they were working as little ladies . . .
> They've left the fame of their shame,
> filled with pretensions, the poor little things!

I've just insinuated that Pedro Bonifacio Palacios, alias Almafuerte, was a thug; now I'll venture to affirm it. A *compadrito* who'd already studied the Last Judgment, which is to say, a glorified and transfigured *compadrito*, in effect a St. Juan Moreira. But a compadre for all that, with the tints of a slum dweller, while possessing a soul of eternity. My opinion does not seek either to cloud his glory or weaken it. I propose it as a way of situating him. I suspect that confessing the *criollo* and suburban aspects of our poet does not make him into a phantom: It adds reality to him, the atmosphere all the dead need, even those who become immortal, and it also adds surprise to him. Insane and almost magic spectacle, that of a *compadrito* who brags (as a thug) of his chastity. Even so, there we have the verses of "In the Abyss," which connect us to him:

> I travel in a fatal straight line
> toward my first desire;
> I don't feel, I don't see
> the walls of that which is real:
> carnal fever never
> darkened my internal light:
> neither because of its ferocity or its tenderness
> has passion left a mark on me . . .
> I feel something like a star
> within the eternal peace!
> I'm a palm tree planted
> on plaster and gravel:

the flowering of pride,
of sublimated pride.
I'm a spore tossed
after the astral procession;
vile plover from the haystack
that flies at the height of an eagle . . .
Shadow of a shadow that desires
to be an immortal shadow!

In the same way, amateur *payadores,* using presumptuous, easily rhymed abstract words, cobble up verses and thus, in rudimentary though comparable verses, I have heard the name of Almafuerte celebrated . . .

Most certainly, Carriego is the day and the night of the *arrabal.* The setting of the suburb belongs to him: The girls with their racket and gossip, the merry-go-rounds on vacant lots, hopscotch, and pride of place on the walkway, the corner—the forum of toughs. Even so, between that day and that night there are crevasses whose passion is too vehement for him and which can't fit into a verse by Carriego. Those crevasses—hardness of sunsets and sunrises, furtive pampa of the west and south, streets that fall apart toward the edge of town—are in the voice of Almafuerte. The desperate voice of Almafuerte.

[1927]   *[AMA]*

THE LANGUAGE
OF THE ARGENTINES

Ladies and gentlemen: Never was equivocation as eloquent as that apocryphal version of me Dr. Arturo Capdevila has just delivered with such benevolent injustice. I want to express to him my gratitude. My completely undeserving self will now attempt (though no one has requested it) to disabuse you with a more true-to-life version. I'm accustomed to writing, not speechmaking, and writing, that lazy artillery pointed toward the invisible, is not a sound apprenticeship for the instantaneous persuasion the orator must have at his disposal. A multiple resignation—yours and mine—is, therefore, advisable.

The language of the Argentines is my subject. That phrase, *the language of the Argentines*, will seem to many an act of mere syntactic mischief, a forced conjoining of two terms lacking any genuine relationship. Something like saying *pure poetry* or *perpetual motion* or *the most ancient historians of the future*. A deception supported by no reality. To that possible observation I will respond in short order. Let's recall that many concepts were in their origin mere verbal accidents that time later confirmed. I suspect that the word *infinite* was at some point an insipid equivalent of *unfinished*; now it is one of the perfections of God in theology, a point of discussion in metaphysics, a literary theme, and an extremely fine concept renewed in mathematics—Russell explains addition and multiplication, the raising to powers of infinite cardinal numbers, and the reasons for their almost terrible dynasties. *Infinite* also confers a true intuition when we look at the sky. At the same time, when the immediate attractions of beauty or a well-cared-for memory of it are upon us, who hasn't felt that the words of praise that preexist are like prophecies of it, like movements of the heart? The word *pretty* is a foreshadowing of everyone's sweetheart, but only that specific darling. I won't bring up more examples because there are too many.

Two antagonistic influences militate against the existence of an Argentine idiom. The first is from those who imagine that such a language is already prefigured in *arrabalero* and in *sainetes*; another is that of the purists or Spain-imbued who believe in the ability of language and in the impiety or uselessness of renovating it.

Let's consider the first of those errors. *Arrabalero*, if its name is not a lie, is the dialect of the *arrabales* or *orillas*. Therefore it should be the usual form of conversation in Buenos Aires neighborhoods such as Liniers, Saavedra, or San Cristóbal Sur. That conjecture is erroneous: There is no one who doesn't feel that our word *arrabal* is more related to economics than to geography. *Arrabal* is any tenement in the Centro. *Arrabal* is the last corner on Uriburu, with the final wall of the Recoleta cemetery, bitter *compadritos* standing in an entryway, a broken-down store, and the whitened line of low houses waiting in calm expectancy—I don't know if they're waiting for social revolution or the organ-grinder. *Arrabal* are those empty, vacant neighborhoods where Buenos Aires collapses into disorder in the west and where the red flag of auctions—sign of our civil epic about brick kilns, monthly payments, and bribes—reveals the reality of our America.

Arrabal in Parque Patricios is the anger of workers and the setting to words of that anger in shameless newspapers. *Arrabal* is the well-established, hard-to-kill warehouse that persists along Entre Ríos or along Las Heras and the little house that doesn't dare approach the street: Behind its large dark wood door there shines a passageway and a patio filled with plants. *Arrabal* is the secluded low ground of Núñez with zinc rooms, little plank bridges over the water that overflows the ditches, and with an unused cart out in the alley. *Arrabal* is too many heterogeneous things for its meaning never to change.

There is no general dialect among our poor classes, and

Arrabalero is certainly not that dialect. The *criollo* never uses it, women speak it infrequently, the *compadrito* himself exhibits it when obviously and audaciously showing off, strutting his stuff. The vocabulary is miserable: It contains barely twenty terms, and a vicious mob of synonyms complicates it. It's so narrow that authors of *sainetes* who use it have to make up new words. They've cleverly turned to the extremely significant trick of inverting the meaning of ordinary terms. This poverty is natural because *arrabalero* is nothing more than a decanting or diffusion of *lunfardo*, which is the secret argot of thieves.

Lunfardo is the vocabulary of a certain sector of society, like so many others. It's the technology of the *furca* (distractions employed by pickpockets) and the *ganzúa* (lock pick). To imagine that this technical language—a specialized language of infamy devoid of words for general usage—can overwhelm Castilian is like dreaming that the dialect of mathematics or locksmithing can rise up to become the only language. English hasn't been obliterated by slang, the Spanish of Spain wasn't overwhelmed by the thieves' argot of the past or by the gypsy-influenced slang of today—a slang that is abundant since it derives from gypsy language and from the addition of one of its variants to the argot of the Spanish criminal world circa 1600.

Arrabalero, besides, is so lacking in soul, so accidental, that the two classical literary figures of our suburbs could do without it. It was not favored either by the poet from Entre Ríos, José Sixto Álvarez, or the man from Entre Ríos—"part joker, part sad"—who continues to collaborate in all the memories of Palermo, the genial boy Carriego. Both knew *lunfardo* and both sidestepped it: Álvarez, in his *Memoirs of a Policeman*, published in 1897, explained many of its terms and usages; Carriego amused himself by using it as a joke he then abstained from signing. The fact is that the two of them believed that *lunfardo* is no good either for the mischief of *criollo* fun or for modest piety. Neither did don Francisco A. Sicardi, in that infinite, muddy, and hurricanelike *Strange Book* of his.

But why go on accumulating illustrious examples? The people of Buenos Aires, hardly fastidious in terms of linguistic correctness, never made verses in that jargon. The *milongas*, the aggressive and wayward voice of the *compadritos*, did not frequent it. This is natural because the neighborhood *compadritos*—the mule driver, worker, or butcher hanging around on corners along those streets in Balvanera or Montserrat—were one thing, and the outlaws who did their dark work in the Bajo de Palermo or out toward La Quema quite another.

The first tangos, the old, wonderful tangos, never had *lunfardo* lyrics: This use of *lunfardo* is merely an affectation that novelty-seeking, contemporary simplemindedness makes obligatory, and which fills tangos with phony secrets and false emphases. Every new tango written in this so-called popular idiom is a puzzle susceptible to diverse readings, with corollaries, dark passages, and the documented discussion of commentators. That obscurity is logical: The common people don't have to add local color to themselves. The faker imagines he does need it, and it's a habit that fits in with his modus operandi. The soul of the *orillas* combined with a vocabulary that belonged to everyone: That was the substance of the snappy *milonga*; international banality and an underworld vocabulary are what we have in today's tango.

I won't flog a dead horse. If the cause is good and won beforehand, the superfluous accumulation of evidence is a harmful custom and makes acquired or recovered truth into a commonplace. To lecture for the sake of lecturing about the almost universality of our language and then to hide in an untamed and suspicious dialect—a jargon of infamy, a prison and tenement argot that transforms us into reverse hypocrites, hypocrites of the underworld and ruination—is a project better suited to the ill-humored and complaining. That program of tragic smallness was rejected already by de Vedia, by Miguel Cané, by Quesada, by Costa Alvarez, by Groussac. This last ironically quipped, "Shall we reject the Spanish caravel in the name of some low-down trick?"

Now I want to set aside *arrabalero* and comment on a different error, that which postulates the perfection of our language and the impious uselessness of refashioning it. Its greatest and only argument consists of the sixty thousand words contained in our dictionary and that of the Spaniards. I suggest that this numerical superiority is an advantage in appearance only, that it is not essential, and that the only infinite language—that of mathematics—is content with a dozen signs in order not to allow itself to be outrun by any single number. That is, the algorithmic dictionary of a single page—with numbers, dashes, crosses—is virtually the richest there is. The number of representations is what matters, not the number of signs. This is an arithmetic superstition, pedantry, the concern of collectors and stamp aficionados.

We know that the Anglican Bishop Wilkins, the most intelligent utopian in terms of language who ever thought, planned a system of international writing or symbols that with only 2,040 signs on pentagram-designed paper could inventory any reality. This silent music of his, of course, did not necessarily involve any sound. That is a maximum advantage, and even though I'd like to go on talking about it, it is the so-called richness of Castilian that must attract me now.

The richness of Spanish is another euphemistic name for its death. Louts and those who aren't louts open our dictionary and are dazzled by the myriad words there that are in no one's mouth. There is no reader, no matter how much of a reader he may be, who is not convinced of his own ignorance looking through those pages. The accumulative criterion behind those pages—which persists in loading onto the Academy's lexicon the entire corpus of argot, of heraldry, all archaisms—has gathered up these dead. The totality is a deliberate necrological spectacle and constitutes "our envied treasure of picturesque, felicitous, and expressive terms." That trinity of pseudo-words—spoken with no degree of precision and only justifiable because of the reigning vainglorious setting—belongs to the purest unspeaking style of those academics.

What they want is perfect synonymity, the Hispanic sermon. The maximum verbal parade, even if populated by ghosts, absences, or the dead. The lack of expression matters not at all; what does matter are the ornaments, jewels, and riches of Spanish, which by another name is called fraud. Mental dreaminess and the acoustic conception of style are the things that foment synonyms: words that without the discomfort of changing

an idea, change noise. The Academy adopts them enthusiastically. Allow me to repeat their recommendation: The abundance
and variety of words (it says) was so highly regarded in our
golden age that the preceptists never tired of recommending it.
If any grammarian, let's say, had to follow the advice of Nebrija,
he would rarely repeat the same word, varying it elegantly in this
or a similar way: "Thus Nebrija asserts, thus he feels it, thus he
teaches, thus he says it, advises it thus, such is his opinion, such
his point of view, such his judgment, as it pleases Nebrija, if we
believe the Spanish Ennius, or employing other terms no less
wise or opportune" (*Grammar of the Academy*, Part II, Chapter 7). I really believe that this mass of equivalences is a resource
as alien to literature as possessing legible handwriting. Besides,
the fallible magnificence of synonyms is embraced so warmly by
the Academy that it sees them even where they don't exist, so
instead of saying *hacerse ilusiones* (to build up one's hopes), an
expression it condemns as a solecism for reasons I can't fathom, it
suggests we use metaphors from blacksmithing (*forjarse ilusiones or chimeras* [forge hopes or chimeras]) or from sleepwalking:
hallucinate, dream while awake.

To affirm an already achieved plenitude for Spanish is illogical
and immoral. It is illogical because the perfection of a language
would postulate either that a great thought or all thinking is very
poor if not carried out in English or German, whose dictionaries
hoard more than one hundred thousand words each. The test is
always carried out with French—a test in which there is a trick,
because the lexical brevity of that language is a salvation and
was stimulated by its rhetoricians. Restrictive or not, Racine's
small vocabulary is deliberate. It's austerity, not indigence.

I want to summarize these thoughts. I see two linguistic
behaviors in writers from these parts. First, that of the *sainete-
ros*, who write in a language no one speaks. It occasionally
gives pleasure because of its exaggerated, caricaturelike air, because of how foreign it sounds. The second is the linguistic
behavior of cultured people, who die the borrowed death of
Spanish. Both diverge from ordinary language: The first imitate
the underworld dictionary, the second that of the memorious
and problematic Spanish of the dictionaries. Equidistant from

their copies, the unwritten Argentine language continues *to speak us*, that is, the language of our passion, of our homes, of shared confidences, of conversational friendship.

Our elders did it better. The tone of their writing was that of their voices: Their mouths were not the contradiction of their hands. They were dignified Argentines: Their calling themselves *criollos* was not *orillero* arrogance or ill humor. They wrote the normal dialect of their days, and they preferred not to fall back on being Spaniards or degenerating into thugs. I'm thinking about Esteban Echeverría, Domingo Faustino Sarmiento, Vicente Fidel López, Lucio V. Mansilla, and Eduardo Wilde. They expressed themselves well in Argentine, a thing that's fallen out of use. They did not need to disguise themselves as something else or pretend to be newly arrived to this territory in order to write.

Nowadays, that naturalness is spent. Two opposing ways of thinking, the pseudoplebeian and the pseudo-Spanish, control today's writing. He who doesn't play the thug to write or turn into a farmhand, bandit, or bravo tries to Spanishize himself or uses a gaseous, abstracted, international Spanish bereft of a homeland. The singular exceptions that remain—Eduardo Schiaffino, Güiraldes—are of the kind that bring us honor. The fact is, of course, a symptom. To be an Argentine in the fighting days of our founding was most certainly not a happy thing: It was a mission. It was a need to create a fatherland, a beautiful risk that contained, for being risky, an element of pride.

Nowadays, being Argentine is the easiest thing in the world. No one even dreams we have something to do. To pass unnoticed, to beg forgiveness for that low-down tango, to be skeptical of all fervor in the French style, and not to get excited about anything is what many aspire to. To play the part of a member of the *Mazorca* or of a Quechua speaker is a masquerade alien to us. But being Argentine should be much more than a suppression or a spectacle. It should be a vocation.

Many, intending to sow doubt, will ask: What abyss separates the Spanish of the Spaniards and our Argentine conversation? None. A fortunate state of affairs for the general comprehension of our words. There is, to be sure, a shade of difference: a

shade that is discreet enough not to bog down the total circula-
tion of language and clear enough so that we can hear the
nation in it. I'm not thinking here about the several thousand
private words we include and which Spaniards don't understand. I'm thinking about the distinct environment of our voice,
about the ironic or tender value we give to certain words in
their unequal tenor.

We haven't changed the intrinsic meaning of words, but we
have altered their connotation. This divergence, of no importance in contentious or didactic prose, is huge with regard to
emotions. Our argumentation may be pan-Hispanic, but our poetry, our humor, are local. The emotive—melancholy or joyful—
belongs to the words, and it's their atmosphere that controls the
emotive, not their meaning. The word *súbdito* (subject)—Arturo
Costa Álvarez again lends it to me—is acceptable in Spain but
denigrating in the New World. The word *enviado* (envied) is a
form of praise in Spain (*envied treasure of picturesque, felicitous, and expressive terms*, as the official grammar of the Spaniards puts it), while here, we think bragging about the envy of
others dreadful.

Our greatest words in poetry, *arrabal* and *pampa*, are felt by
no Spaniard. Our term *lindo* (beautiful) is a word that is total
praise; among the Spaniards it is not so overwhelmingly ap-
proving. *Gozar* (enjoy) and *sobrar* (dominate) have bad intentions here. The word *egregio* (eminent), used so much by the
Revista de Occidente and even by don Américo Castro, does
not impress us. We could go on at length in this vein.

Of course, mere differentiation is a tricky norm. Spanish
terms are no less Argentine than gaucho terms and at times even
more so: The word *llovizna* (drizzle) is as much ours as the
word *garúa* (drizzle), but more ours is the one known by all, the
word *pozo* (well), than the country term *jaguel*. The systematic,
blind preference for native expressions would turn into a new
kind of pedantry: a different error and another kind of bad
taste. This we see with the word *macana* (a club, but also a
blunder or silly idea). Don Miguel de Unamuno—the only Spaniard who understands metaphysics and for that reason, and for
other acts of intelligence, is a great writer—has tended to favor

that term. *Macana*, nevertheless, is a word used by those negligent in thinking. The jurist Segovia, in his hasty *Dictionary of Argentinisms*, writes this: *Macana: Folly, nonsense, silliness.* This, which is already too much, is not enough. *Macana* is what we say to paradoxes; *macana* is our response to madness; *macana* is a setback, a commonplace, our reaction to hyperbole, incongruity, our term for stupidity and foolishness, for what is unusual. It's a word of lazy generalization, which is the source of its success. It's a limit-word used to step back from things we don't understand or don't want to understand. So die, *macana*! Word of our daydreams and our chaos!

In sum, the verbal problem (which is a literary problem as well) is of such a nature that no general or catholic solution can be prescribed for it. Those of us who dwell within the community of language (that is, within the comprehensible, because there is a boundary line between the infinite and what we can't honestly complain about) have the obligation to find our own voices. Of course, writers have that obligation more than anyone else. We, those who attempt the paradox of communication with others by means of words alone—and at that, with words written on paper—know well the shame of our language. We, who have renounced that grand auxiliary dialogue of facial expressions, gestures, and smiles that make up half of any conversation and more than half of its charm, have suffered in our own verbal poverty the stuttering thing it is. We know that it was not the idle gardener Adam, but the Devil—that hissing snake who invented both error and adventure, that abyss within chance; the Devil, that eclipse of an angel—who baptized the things of this world. We know that language is like the moon and has its dark side. We know it all too well, but we would like to make it as limpid as that future which is the greatest possession of the fatherland.

We live in a time of promise. Nineteen hundred and twenty-seven: a great day-before for Argentina. We want the Hispanic language that was serene incredulity in Cervantes and hard-joking in Quevedo, and the appetite for happiness—not felicity—in Fray Luis de León, and nihilism and preaching always to be a blessing and a passion in these lands. May someone declare himself fortunate in the Spanish language; may metaphysical horror in grand style be thought in Spanish. May that someone have either a touch or an abundance of daring.

People were always putting death into that language, always putting in disillusionment, advice, remorse, scruples, and precautions, and when not doing that, they were using it for puns and *calembours*, which are also death. Its very sonority (meaning, that annoying predominance of vowels that, because there are only a few of them, bore us) makes it sermonlike and emphatic. But we would like a docile and felicitous Spanish that would be concordant with the impassioned condition of our sunsets, with the infinite sweetness of our neighborhoods, with the power of our summers, our rains, and our public faith.

The substance of things hoped for, the evidence of things not seen: Thus St. Paul defines faith. A memory that comes to us from the future is how I'd translate it. Hope is our friend, and that full Argentine intonation of Castilian is one of the confirmations that it speaks to us. If everyone expresses his intimate self, we'll have it. Let the heart and the imagination express whatever they contain. We need no philological cleverness.

This is what I wanted to tell you. The future (whose best name is hope) is tugging at our heartstrings.

[1927]   [AMA]

FROM

EVARISTO CARRIEGO

(1930)

BUENOS AIRES: PALERMO

To Paul Groussac we owe the documentation of Palermo's antiquity. He discovered in *The Annals of the Library* (volume Four, p. 360) this proof, which he later published in Number 242 of *Nosotros*. It seems the name Palermo derives from a Sicilian, Domínguez (Domenico), who came to Argentina from Palermo in Italy. Once here, he added Palermo to his own name, perhaps to retain at least one Italian name that could not be Hispanicized. The note adds: "He entered these lands at twenty years of age and is now married to a conquistador's daughter." This Domínguez Palermo, meat supplier to the city between 1605 and 1614, owned a corral, near the Maldonado River, where he penned up and slaughtered stray stock.

The establishment itself has been slaughtered and erased, but we do have a precise reference to "a dapple-gray mule that wanders around Palermo farm, on the outskirts of this city." I see the place, absurdly bright and small, way back in time, and I have no need to add further details. All we have to do is imagine the place all by itself. The jumbled, ever-changing style of reality, punctuated here and there with ironies, surprises, and strange forebodings, themselves surprises, could only be re-created by writing a novel, which I'm not going to attempt. Fortunately, the style of the realist novel is not the only one there is. We can also turn to the past itself, whose essence is not the proliferation of events, but the arbitrary creation of cherished images as well as the destruction of many others. This is the natural poetry of our ignorance, and I will seek no other.

A rough sketch of Palermo would include the modest farm

and the filthy slaughter yard. We would add, to flesh out those sleepy nights, one or two launches run aground by Dutch smugglers and hidden in the cattails. To recover every detail of that almost immobile prehistory would mean weaving a senseless chronicle of infinitesimal processes: the stages of the distracted, secular advance of Buenos Aires over Palermo, which at the time was made up of vague plots of land, occasionally underwater with their back turned toward the rest of the country. The most direct means to evoke all that, following the cinematic method, would be to propose a series of discontinuous images: a team of mules delivering wine, the unbroken mules blindfolded; willow leaves floating in a calm and long spread of water; a staggering waterbird hanging over his stilts, wading through the torrential drains; the open country standing idle; the determined tracks of a herd heading to the stockyards in the North; a cowhand (outlined against the rising sun) who dismounts his exhausted horse and slits its wide neck; smoke that fades in the air.

That was how Palermo was until don Juan Manuel de Rosas came along to re-create it. Rosas is the mythological father of Palermo—not a merely historic father like that Domínguez-Domenico discovered by Groussac. The foundation was carried out by main force. Rosas would have found on his arrival a sweet old-time farmhouse on the road to Barracas, a common enough phenomenon at the time. But Rosas wanted to build, wanted his house to be his own child, not saturated with unknown foreign lives. Thousands of wagonloads of black earth were brought from "Rosas's alfalfa fields" (later Belgrano) to level and enrich the original clayish soil, until the savage, ungrateful mud of Palermo conformed to his will.

Around 1840, Palermo rose to be the ruling head of the Republic and became the site of the dictator's court, a curse word for the *unitarios*. I won't reveal that history in order not to eclipse the rest. Just let me enumerate "that great whitewashed house called his Palace" (Hudson, *Far Away and Long Ago*, 108) and the orange grove and the pool with brick walls and wrought-iron railings where the Restorer's boat ventured on a voyage so frugal that Schiaffino commented:

Aquatic jaunts in such shallow water must have provided little pleasure, and, in such reduced spaces, were like midget sailing. But Rosas was calm; looking up, he could see outlined against the sky the silhouettes of guards posted against the railing, scrutinizing the horizon like birds of prey.

That court quickly disintegrated into slums: the stooped-over Hernández Division encampment, made of crude adobes, and the Palermo Barracks settlement that was the scenario of the fights and passions of dark women. The neighborhood, as you see, was always a two-sided playing card, a two-faced coin.

That dazzling Palermo lasted twelve years in the anguish of the demanding presence of an obese blond man who traveled the brand-new roads wearing blue military trousers, red braiding, a scarlet vest, and a broad-brimmed hat. Rosas was in the habit of waving a long reed he held like a scepter as light as air. One afternoon, that immortal man left Palermo to command the debacle, a battle lost before it was fought, at Caseros. Justo José, the other Rosas, entered Palermo with the impudence of a wild bull, wearing the narrow scarlet ribbon of the Mazorca on his clownish hat and the lavish uniform of a general. He entered, and if Ascasubi's heavy-handed pamphlets don't mislead us:

> at the entrance to Palermo
> he ordered to be hung
> two unfortunate men,
> who after being shot
> were strung from the *ombú* trees
> until from there, bit by bit,
> they rotted away . . .

Ascasubi then takes note of the idle troops from Entre Ríos in the grand army:

> Meanwhile, in the quagmire
> of Palermo, huddled together,
> almost all of them shirtless,

were his men from Entre Ríos
(as he says) miserable,
eating skinny calves
and selling off the leftovers . . .

Thousands of days unknown to memory, misty zones of time, grew and wasted away until, after new construction—the Penitentiary in 1877, the Norte Hospital in 1882, and the Rivadavia Hospital in 1887—we reach Palermo just before 1890, when the Carriego family bought a house there. It's about that Palermo of 1889 that I want to write. I will tell what I know without constraint, omitting nothing, because life is as modest as a crime, and we don't know what God thinks the important things are. Besides, circumstantial details always have pathos.[1] I write everything and risk writing all-too-familiar truths, but a greater risk would be to lose them, as carelessness is both the first face and poorest form of mystery.[2]

Beyond the branch of the Western Railroad that went through

---

[1] "The pathetic, almost always, consists in the detail of little circumstances," observes Gibbon in one of the last notes of Chapter 50 of his *Decline and Fall* (note 179 in the Penguin edition, vol. III, p. 227). [AMA]

[2] I assert—without exaggerated fear or newfangled love of paradox—that only new nations have a past, that is, the autobiographical memory of that past; that is, they have living history. If time is successive, we should recognize that where there is the greatest density of events, more time runs, and that the powerful sea belongs to this inconsequential side of the world. The conquest and colonization of these realms—fearful forts of clay stuck on the coast and from the horizon noticed by the shooting bows of the tribes—were of such ephemeral operation that a grandfather of mine, in 1872, could command the last important battle against the Indians, carrying out during the second half of the nineteenth century the conquering work of the sixteenth. Nevertheless, why bring up already dead destinies? I have not felt the weightlessness of time in Granada, in the shadow of towers hundreds of times more ancient than the fig trees, while I have on Pampa and Triunvirato: insipid place of English flagstones now, of beautiful brick kilns three years ago, of chaotic horse yards five years ago. Time—a European emotion of men plentiful in days and thus their vindication and crown—circulates more impudently in these republics. The young, to their detriment, feel it. Here we are of the same time as time; we are its brothers.

the area called Centro América, the neighborhood idled away
its time amid the banners of auctioneers, not only on the
elemental plain but on the farms torn to shreds, brutally
broken down into lots and then trampled by shops, coal-yards,
backyards, tenements, barbershops, and warehouses. Gardens
remained, the degenerate and mutilated relic of a grand estate,
drowned by the neighborhood, the kind with insane palm trees
growing amid rusted scrap iron and building junk.

Palermo was carefree poverty. The fig tree darkened on the
wall; the modest little balconies faced monotonous days; the
lost horn of the peanut vendor explored the sunsets. Looking
into those humble houses, you might see the odd makeshift
planter aridly crowned with prickly pears. This sinister plant,
which in the universal sleep of others seems to belong to the
land of nightmares, is really a long-suffering plant that lives in
the harshest soils and the desert air and which, absentmindedly,
people consider decorative. There was happiness as well: the
flower bed in the patio, the hoodlum's rhythmic walk, the bal-
ustrade whose columns reveal patches of sky.

The stained, greenish horse and its Garibaldi did not depress
the *portones* of yesteryear. (The malady is general: Nowadays,
there isn't a square that doesn't suffer its bronze thug.) The
botanical garden, a silent shipyard of trees, preferred site for
taking walks in the capital, formed a corner with the dismantled
dirt plaza. But not the zoo, referred to then as "the beasts,"
because in those days it was located further to the north. Now
(smell of caramel and tiger) it occupies the place where, eighty
years ago, a racket was made by the neighborhood called
Cuartos de Palermo. Only a few streets—Serrano, Canning,
Coronel—were frighteningly paved, with the intervention of
smooth trotters for the wagons, impressive as a parade for
showy victories.

The number sixty-four, an obliging vehicle that shares with
the powerful, earlier shadow of don Juan Manuel, the creation
of Palermo, makes its way uphill along Godoy Cruz Street.
The driver, his visor on one side, with his *milonga*-playing
horn, aroused the neighborhood's admiration or emulation, but
the conductor—a professional doubter of every passenger's

honesty—was a fought-against institution, so of course there would have to be the compadre who stuck his ticket into his fly, repeating indignantly that if they wanted it, all they had to do was take it.

I'll seek more noble realities. To the east, toward the border of Balvanera, there are many large, yellow or brown houses with arched doors—their arches repeated in mirrorlike fashion by the entryways facing them—and with a delicate outer door made of wrought iron. When the impatient nights of October drew chairs and people out to the sidewalk, the narrow houses allowed the visitor to see all the way to the back, and there was yellow light in the patios, the street was confidential and light, and the empty houses were like lanterns all lined up.

I remember that impression of unreality and serenity most clearly in a story or symbol that seems always to have been with me. It's an instant ripped out of a story I heard in a store, and it's both trivial and complicated. I recover it with some uncertainty. The hero of this half-forgotten odyssey was the eternal *criollo* being chased by the police, betrayed this time by a deformed and hateful man who nevertheless had a peerless guitar.

The story, the salvaged piece of the story, tells how the hero managed to escape from jail, how he had to get his revenge in a single night, how he searched in vain for the traitor, how as he wandered the moonlit streets, the worn-out breeze brought him hints of the guitar, how he followed that trail through the labyrinths and vagaries of the wind, how he turned and turned again the corners of Buenos Aires, how he reached the distant threshold where the traitor was playing the guitar, how he made his way through the audience, impaled him with his knife, how he left in a daze, leaving both the informer and his guitar dead and silent.

Toward the sunset stood the gringo misery of the neighborhood, its nakedness. The term *las orillas*—riverbanks—fits these odd places with supernatural precision, where the earth becomes as indeterminate as the sea and seems worthy of illustrating Shakespeare's insinuation, "The earth hath bubbles as the water has." Toward the sunset there were dusty alleys that became poorer and poorer as they moved outward from the afternoon;

there were places where a shed belonging to the railroad or an empty space overgrown with agaves or an almost confidential breeze inaugurated (badly) the pampa. Or rather one of those houses devoid of stucco with a low, barred window, sometimes with a yellow rug (with figures) in the back, the kind that the solitude of Buenos Aires seems to nurture, with no visible human participation. After that: the Maldonado, a dried-up, yellow ditch stretching itself with no destiny whatsoever from Chacarita cemetery and which, because of a horrifying miracle, went from being dead of thirst to the insane lengths of violent water that washed away the dying settlement of houses on the *orillas*.

Some fifty years ago, after that irregular ditch or death, the sky began, a sky of whinnies and manes and sweetgrass, a horse heaven, a lazy happy hunting ground for the police department's retired horses. Toward the Maldonado the native thugs became thin on the ground, replaced by Calabrians, people with whom no one wanted any trouble because of the dangerous good memory of their rage, because of the traitorous knife thrusts that could come much later. That's where Palermo grew sad, because the iron rails of the Pacific line followed the stream, releasing that peculiar sadness of enslaved, big things, a sadness of high barriers like the raised shaft of a cart at rest, of the erect embankments and sidings. A borderland of working smoke, a borderland of brutish cars in motion, closed off that side. Behind, the stream either grew or flared up.

Nowadays they're imprisoning it: The almost infinite flank of solitude that remained unknown just a while ago, around the corner from the cardsharp's tea shop, "La Paloma," will soon be replaced by a silly street with English paving stones. Of the Maldonado, nothing will remain except our memory, tall and alone, and the best Argentine *sainete* and the two tangos with that title: one primitive, a present untroubled moment, a mere plan for dancing, the opportunity to give oneself over completely to the *cortes*—tango "cuts"; the other a sorrowful tango—a song in the style of the Boca southside neighborhood—and the odd, lowly cliché that will not evoke the essential, the impression of space and a mistaken other life in the imagination of those who did not live it.

Thinking about it now, I don't think the Maldonado was different from other dirt-poor areas, but the idea of its low-life mob, acting outrageously in broken-down bordellos, in the shadow of floods and the area's demise, was powerful in the popular imagination. Thus, in the dexterous *sainete* I mentioned, the stream isn't just a helpful backdrop, it's a presence much more important than Nava the Black and Dominga the Tart, and the Puppet. (Puente Alsina, with its not-yet-scarred-over yesterday of knife fights and its memory of the grand uprising of 1880, is displacing it in the mythology of Buenos Aires. With regard to reality, it's easy to see that the poorest neighborhoods are usually the most timid and that a terrified sense of middle-class decency flourishes in them.)

It was alongside the stream that the great land storms that darkened the day began, as well as the *pampero*'s great gust, which pounded at all the doors facing south and left a thistle in the *zaguán* along with the all-devouring cloud of locusts that tried to scare people by screaming,[3] as well as solitude and rain. That *orilla* had the taste of dust.

Toward the treacherous water of the river, toward the forest, the neighborhood grew hard. The first structure at that end was the Northside slaughter yard, which took up about eighteen blocks bordered by these future streets: Anchorena, Las Heras, Austria, and Beruti—now with no other verbal relic than the name *la Tablada* (stalls at the slaughteryard), which I heard a cart driver cry, ignorant of its old meaning. I've induced the reader to imagine that huge area of many blocks: The corrals disappeared in 1870, but even so, the figure is typical of the place, always crisscrossed by farms—the cemetery, the Rivadavia Hospital, the jail, the market, the municipal square, the present wool-washing plant, the brewery, Hale's farm—shrouded by the poverty of beaten-down destinies. That farm was famous for two reasons: for the pear trees the local kids raided in clandestine mobs and for the ghost who visited Aguero Street, its

---

3 Destroying them is the work of heretics because they bear the sign of the cross, the mark of their special emission and division by the Lord.

impossible head resting on the arm of a lantern. Because to the real dangers of knife-wielding compadres, we must add the fantastic dangers of a mythology on the run. The *widow* and the *tin hog*, as sordid as the lowlands, were the most feared creatures in that sordid neighborhood's religion. The north had always been the place where trash was burned, and so it's only natural that the garbage of souls would float in its air. There are poor street corners that don't fall down only because they're held in place by dead *compadritos*.

Strolling along Chavango Street (later renamed Las Heras)—the last bar on the road was named The First Light because of the district's early-rising habits—leaves an impression, proper at that, of clogged dead-end streets without people, and, finally, after the fatigue of walking, a human light in a store. Within the depths of the red cemetery of the North and the Penitentiary, a smashed-up suburb of low, unstuccoed buildings has materialized from the dust, infamously known as Tierra del Fuego. Rubble at its threshold, street corners of solitude or aggression, furtive men who call out to one another and name one another's character, who scatter suddenly in the lateral light of the alleys. The entire neighborhood was a final corner. Thugs on horseback, Mitre-style brimmed hats over their eyes and in countrified *bombachas,* out of inertia or impulse, kept up a war of individual duels with the police.

The weapon of the *orillero* fighter, without being very long—it was the pride of the brave to use knives with short blades—was made of better material than the machete acquired by the state, that is, the state's machete cost more and was made of inferior materials. It was guided by an arm more desirous of knocking over, one that knew better the direction of the instantaneous turns of the fight. Merely for the viscosity of its rhyme, a bit of that fighting has withstood forty years of forgetting:

> Out of the way, I beg you,
> 'Cause I'm from Tierra'el Juego.[4]

---

4   Taullard, 33. [AMA]

That frontier, let me note, was not only one of fights but of guitars as well.

As I write down these recovered facts, the grateful verse of Browning's "Home-Thoughts" seeks me out with apparent arbitrariness: "Here and here did England help me." Browning wrote these words thinking about an abnegation at sea and the tall, sculpted ship like a chess piece upon which Nelson fell. Repeated by me—translated as well the name of the homeland, since for Browning his England was no less immediate—it serves as a symbol of my solitary nights and ecstatic, eternal walks through the infinite neighborhoods. Because Buenos Aires is deep, and never have I, disillusioned or suffering, given myself over to its streets without receiving some unexpected consolation, whether from feeling unreality, from guitars at the back of some patio, or from contact with other lives. "Here and here did England help me": here and here did Buenos Aires help me. This is one of the reasons I decided to compose this chapter.

[1930]   [AMA]

A HISTORY OF THE TANGO

Vicente Rossi, Carlos Vega, and Carlos Muzzio Sáenz Pena, each a diligent historian, have all investigated the origins of the tango. I must say that I subscribe to all of their conclusions—as well as to others. There is also a history of the tango that the cinema periodically divulges; according to this sentimental version, the tango was born in the riverbank tenements of Buenos Aires (the Boca, by virtue of the area's photogenic features); the upper classes rejected it at first but, around 1910, indoctrinated by the good example of Paris, finally threw open their doors to that interesting product of the slums. This "from rags to riches" *Bildungsroman* is by now a sort of incontestable or proverbial truth; my memories (and I am over fifty) and my own informal inquiries by no means support such a version.

I have spoken to José Saborido, who wrote "Felicia" and "La morocha" [The Brunette] with Ernesto Poncio (who also wrote the tango "Don Juan"); to the brothers of Vicente Greco, author of "La viruta" [The Woodchip] and "La tablada" [The Wooden Board]; to Nicolás Paredes (once the political boss of Palermo), and to a few gaucho ballad singers he knew. I let them talk; I carefully avoided formulating questions that might suggest determined answers. The derivations of the tango, the topography, and even the geography they related were singularly diverse: Saborido (a Uruguayan) preferred a Montevidean cradle on the east bank; Poncio (from Retiro) opted for Buenos Aires and for his own neighborhood; those from the Southside docks invoked the Calle Chile; those from the northern part of town, the raucous Calle Temple or the Calle Junín.

In spite of the divergences I have enumerated, which could be easily multiplied by asking people from La Plata or from around Rosario, my advisers agree on one essential fact, that the tango was born in the brothels. (And also on the date of its origins, which none felt was much before 1880 or after 1890.) The primitive instrumentation of its earliest orchestras—piano, flute, violin, and later the concertina—confirms, with its extravagance, the evidence that the tango did not arise from the riverbank slums where, as everyone knows, the six strings of the guitar were sufficient. Other confirmations also abound—the lascivious movements, the obvious connotations of certain titles ("El choclo" [The Corn-cob], "El fierrazo" [The Iron Rod]), and what I observed as a boy in Palermo and, years later, in La Chacarita and Boedo: that on the street corners pairs of men would dance, since the women of the town would not want to take part in such lewd debauchery. Evaristo Carriego portrayed it in his *Misas herejes* [Heathen Masses]:

> *En la calle, la buena gente derrocha*
> *sus guarangos decires más lisonjeros,*
> *porque al compás de un tango, que es "La morocha,"*
> *lucen ágiles cortes dos orilleros.*

[The gentlefolk on the street lavish / their rude flattery, / because to the beat of a tango about a dark-eyed girl, / two men from the slums dance light-footed steps in a lewd embrace.]

On another page, with a wealth of poignant details, Carriego depicts a humble wedding party; the groom's brother is in jail; two rowdy boys are itching for a fight, and the neighborhood tough has to pacify them with threats; there is mistrust, ill feeling, and horseplay, but

> *El tío de la novia, que se ha creído*
> *obligado a fijarse si el baile toma*
> *buen carácter, afirma, medio ofendido:*
> *que no se admiten cortes, ni aun en broma.*
> *Que, la modestia a un lado, no se la pega*

ninguno de esos vivos . . . seguramente.
La casa será pobre, nadie lo niega:
todo lo que se quiera, pero decente.

[The bride's uncle takes it upon himself / to see that the dancing stays proper though festive. / There'll be no slithering tangos here, he says, / nothing suggestive, not even in fun. / All modesty aside, not that these louts would / understand, this house may be poor—no denying that— / whatever you say, but / one thing at least, it's respectable.]

The momentary glimpse of the strict uncle, which the two stanzas capture, highlights people's first reaction to the tango—"that reptile from the brothel," as Lugones would define it with laconic contempt (*El payador*, 117). It took many years for the Northside to compel the tenements to adopt the tango—by then made respectable by Paris, of course—and I am not sure that this has been completely successful. What was once a devilish orgy is now a way of walking.

THE FIGHTING TANGO

The sexual nature of the tango has often been noted, but not so its violence. Certainly both are modes or manifestations of the same impulse; in all the languages I know, the word for "man" connotes both sexual potency and combative potential, and the word *virtus*, Latin for "courage," comes from *vir*, meaning "male." Similarly, an Afghan on a page in *Kim* states flatly—as if the two acts were essentially one—"When I was fifteen, I had shot my man and begot my man."

To speak of the "fighting tango" is not strong enough; I would say that the tango and the *milonga* directly express a conviction that poets have often tried to voice with words: that a fight can be a celebration. In the famous *History of the Goths* that Jordanes wrote in the sixth century, we read that Attila, before his defeat at Châlons, harangued his armies, telling them that fortune had reserved for them "the joys of this battle" ("*certaminis hujus gaudia*"). The *Iliad* speaks of Achaeans for whom war was sweeter than returning home in hollowed ships to their beloved native land, and relates how Paris, son of Priam, ran with rapid feet into battle like a stallion with flowing mane in pursuit of mares. In *Beowulf*—the Saxon epic that launched the Germanic literatures—the bard calls battle a "*sweorda gelac*" or "game of swords." Scandinavian poets of the eleventh century called it the "Vikings' feast." In the early seventeenth century, Quevedo, in one of his ballads, called a duel a "dance of swords"—almost the same as the anonymous Anglo-Saxon's "game of swords." In his splendid evocation of the Battle of Waterloo, Hugo said that the soldiers, realizing they were going to die in that festivity ("*comprenant qu'ils allaient mourir dans cette fête*"), saluted their god (the Emperor) standing amid the storm.

These examples, recorded in the course of my random readings, could be effortlessly multiplied; in the *Chanson de Roland* or in Ariosto's vast poem there are similar passages. Any of those mentioned here—Quevedo's or the one about Attila, let us say— are undeniably effective. All of them, nonetheless, suffer from the original sin of literariness: they are structures of words, forms made of symbols. "Dance of swords," for example, invites us to link two dissimilar images in order for "dance" to imbue "combat" with joy, but it does not speak directly to our blood, does not re-create such joy in us. Schopenhauer (*Welt als Wille und Vorstellung* I, 52) has written that music is as near to us as the world itself; without the world, without a common stock of memories summoned by language, there would be no literature, but music does not need, could exist, without the world. Music is will and passion; the old tango, as music, immediately transmits that joy of combat which Greek and German poets, long ago, tried to express in words. Certain composers today strive for that heroic tone and sometimes conceive competent *milongas* about the Bateria slums or the Barrio Alto, but their labors— with deliberately old-fashioned lyrics and music—are exercises in nostalgia for what once was, laments for what is now lost, intrinsically sad even when their melody is joyful. They are to the rough and innocent *milongas* in Rossi's book what *Don Segundo Sombra* is to *Martín Fierro* or to *Paulino Lucero*.

We read in one of Oscar Wilde's dialogues that music reveals a personal past which, until then, each of us was unaware of, moving us to lament misfortunes we never suffered and wrongs we did not commit. For myself, I confess that I cannot hear "El Marne" or "Don Juan" without remembering in detail an apocryphal past, simultaneously stoic and orgiastic, in which I have challenged and fought, in the end to fall silently, in an obscure knife fight. Perhaps this is the tango's mission: to give Argentines the belief in a brave past, in having met the demands of honor and bravery.

A PARTIAL MYSTERY

Having accepted the tango's compensatory function, we still have a small mystery to resolve. South America's independence was, to a great extent, an Argentine enterprise. Argentine men fought in battles all over the continent: in Maipù, in Ayacucho, in Junín. Then came the civil wars, the war in Brazil, the campaigns against Rosas and Urquizas, the war in Paraguay, the frontier war with the Indians. . . . Our military past is populous, but, indisputably, though Argentines consider themselves brave, they do not identify with that past (despite the bias in schools in favor of the study of history), but rather with the vast generic figures of the Gaucho and the Hoodlum. If I am not mistaken, this instinctual paradox has an explanation: the Argentine finds his symbol in the gaucho and not the soldier because the courage ascribed to the former by oral tradition is not in the service of a cause but rather is pure. The gaucho and the hoodlum are seen as rebels; Argentines, unlike North Americans and most Europeans, do not identify with the state. This can be attributed to the fact that the state is an inconceivable abstraction.[1] The Argentine is an individual, not a citizen; to him, aphorisms

---

1 The state is impersonal; the Argentine thinks only in terms of personal relationships. For him, therefore, stealing public monies is not a crime. I am stating the fact, not justifying or condoning it.

such as Hegel's "The State is the reality of the moral idea" are sinister jokes. Films made in Hollywood repeatedly intend for us to admire the case of a man (usually a newspaper reporter) who befriends a criminal in order to turn him in to the police; Argentines, for whom friendship is a passion and the police a mafia, consider such a "hero" to be an incomprehensible scoundrel. Along with Don Quixote, the Argentine feels that "up there, each man will have to answer for his own sins" and that "an honest man should not be the hangmen of others, with whom he has nothing to do" (*Don Quixote* I, 22). When faced, more than once, with the empty symmetries of Spanish style, I have thought that we differ irredeemably from Spain; these lines from the *Quixote* are enough to convince me of my error. They are the secret, quiet symbol of an affinity. One night in Argentine literature confirms this affinity, that desperate night when a rural police sergeant exclaimed he would not commit the crime of killing a brave man and began to fight against his own soldiers, together with the deserter Martín Fierro.

THE LYRICS

Uneven in quality, as they conspicuously proceed from hundreds and thousands of diversely inspired or merely industrious pens, the lyrics of the tango, after half a century, now constitute an almost impenetrable *corpus poeticum* which historians of Argentine literature will read or, in any case, defend. Popular culture, when the people no longer understand it, when the years have made it antiquated, gains the nostalgic veneration of scholars and validates polemics and glossaries. By 1990, the suspicion or certainty may arise that the true poetry of our time is not in Banchs's *La urna* [The Urn] or Mastronardi's *Luz de provincia* [Provincial Light] but rather those imperfect pieces conserved in the songbook *El alma que canta* [The Singing Soul]. Such a conjecture is melancholy. A culpable negligence has kept me from acquiring and studying this chaotic repertory, but I am not unacquainted with its variety and the growing compass of its themes. At the beginning the tango had no lyrics,

or else they were obscene and haphazard. Some were rustic—
"*Yo soy la fiel compañera / del noble gaucho porteño*" [I am the
girlfriend, ever true/of the noble dockside city gaucho]—
because their composers sought a popular flavor, but the low
life and the slums were not poetic material, then. Others, like
the related dance, the *milonga*,[2] were jolly, showy fanfare: "*En
el tango soy tan taura / que cuando hago un doble corte / corre
la voz por el Norte / si es que me encuentro en el Sur*" [When I
tango I'm so tough / that, when I whirl a double cut / word
reaches the Northside / if I'm dancing in the South]. Later, the
genre chronicled, like certain French naturalist novels or certain
Hogarth engravings, the local perils of the "harlot's progress":
"*Luego fuiste la amiguita / de un viejo boticario / y el hijo de
un comisario / todo el vento te sacó*" [Next you became the
mistress / of an old pharmacist / and the police chief's son /
knocked the wind out of your sails]. Still later, the deplorable gentrification of rough or rundown neighborhoods, like
"*Puente Alsina, / ¿dónde está ese malevaje?*" [Puente Alsina, /
where are all your hooligans?] or "*¿Dónde están aquellos hombres y esas chinas, / vinchas rojas y chambergos que Requena
conoció? / ¿Dónde está mi Villa Crespo de otros tiempos? / Se
vinieron los judíos, Triunvirato se acabó*" [Where are those
men and their gals / those red bandannas and slouch bats that
Requena once knew? / Where's the Villa Crespo I used to know?
/ Then Jews moved in and the Triumvirato moved on]. From
early on, the woes of secret or sentimental love had kept the
pens busy: "*¿No te acordás que conmigo / te pusistes un som-
brero / y aquel cinturón de cuero / que a otra mina la afané?*"
[Remember when, with me / you wore that hat, and more, /
around your waist that leather belt / I'd swiped from another
broad?]. Tangos of guilt, tangos of hatred, tangos of sarcasm
and bitterness, were written, difficult to transcribe and even to

2 *Yo soy del barrio del Alto, / soy del barrio del Retiro. / Yo soy aquel que
no miro / con quién tengo que pelear, / y a quién, en milonguear, / ninguno se
puso a tiro.* [I'm from the Barrio del Alto, / from the Retiro, I am. / I'm the man
who barely notices / whomever I have to fight, / or whomever I *milonga*, /
nobody fools with me.]

remember. All sides of city life began entering the tango; the low life and the slums were not its only subjects. In the preface to his *Satires*, Juvenal wrote memorably that everything which moved men—desire, fear, anger, carnal pleasure, intrigues, happiness—would be the subject of his book; with excusable exaggeration, we might apply his famous "*quidquid agunt homines*" to the whole of tango lyrics. We might also say that these lyrics form a vast, unconnected *comédie humaine* of Buenos Aires life. At the end of the eighteenth century, Wolf wrote that the *Iliad* was a series of songs and rhapsodies before it became an epic; this knowledge may allow for the prophecy that, in time, tango lyrics will form a long civic poem, or will suggest to some ambitious person the writing of that poem.

Andrew Fletcher's similar statement is well known: "If they let me write all a nation's ballads, I don't care who writes the laws"; the dictum suggests that common or traditional poetry can influence feelings and dictate conduct. The Argentine tango, if we apply this conjecture, might appear as a mirror of our reality and, at the same time, a mentor or model with a certain malignant influence. The first *milongas* and tangos might have been foolish, or at least slipshod, but they were heroic and happy. The later tango is resentful, deplores with sentimental excess one's miseries, and celebrates shamelessly the misfortunes of others.

Around 1926, I remember blaming the Italians (particularly the Genoese in the Boca) for the tango's decline. In that myth, or fantasy, of our "native" tango corrupted by "foreigners," I now see a clear symptom of certain nationalist heresies that later devastated the world—coming from the foreigners, of course. It was not the concertina, which I once ridiculed as contemptible, nor the hardworking composers who made the tango what it is, but the whole republic. Those old "natives" who engendered the tango, moreover, were named Bevilacqua, Greco, de Bassi. . . .

Some may object to my denigration of today's tango, arguing that the transition from boldness or swagger to sadness is not necessarily a bad thing and might even be a sign of maturity. My imagined adversary might well add that the innocent, brave

Ascasubi is to the plaintive Hernández what the first tango is to the latest and that no one—save, perhaps, Jorge Luis Borges—has dared to infer from this diminished happiness that *Martín Fierro* is inferior to *Paulino Lucero*. The answer is easy: the difference is not only in its hedonistic tone but in its moral tone as well. In the everyday tango of Buenos Aires—the tango of family gatherings and respectable tearooms—there is a trivial vulgarity, a taste of infamy that the tango of the knife and the brothel never even suspected.

Musically, the tango is probably not important; its only importance is what we give it. This reflection is correct, but perhaps applies to everything. To our own death, for example, or to the woman who rejects us. . . . The tango can be debated, and we have debates over it, but it still guards, as does all that is truthful, a secret. Dictionaries of music record its short, adequate definition, approved by all; this elementary definition promises no difficulties, but the French or Spanish composer who then follows it and correctly crafts a "tango" is shocked to discover he has constructed something that our ears do not recognize, that our memory does not harbor, and that our bodies reject. We might say that without the evenings and nights of Buenos Aires a tango cannot be made, and that in heaven there awaits us Argentines the Platonic idea of the tango, its universal form (barely spelled out by "La tablada" and "El choclo") a valiant species which, however humble, has its place in the universe.

THE CHALLENGE

There is a legendary or historical account, perhaps both legend and history (which may be another way of saying legendary), that illustrates the cult of courage. Its best written versions can be found in Eduardo Gutierrez's novels, now unjustly forgotten, such as *Hormiga Negra* [Black Ant] or *Juan Moreira*; among its oral versions the first I heard came from a Buenos Aires neighborhood called Tierra del Fuego, bounded by a penitentiary, a river, and a cemetery. The hero of this version was Juan Mu-

raña, wagon driver and knife fighter, in whom converged all the
tales of courage circulating around the docks of the Northside.
A man from Los Corrales or Las Barracas, knowing the fame
of Juan Muraña, whom he has never seen, came up from his
outlying slum in the Southside to pick a fight; he challenged him
in a neighborhood bar, and the two moved out on the street to
fight; each is wounded, but in the end Muraña slashes the man's
face and says to him: "I'm letting you live so that you can come
looking for me again."

The detachment of that duel was engraved on my memory; it
persisted in my conversations (as my friends knew too well);
around 1927, I wrote it down and gave it the deliberately
laconic title "Men Fought"; years later the anecdote helped me
come up with a providential story—since it was hardly a good
one—called "Street Corner Man"; in 1950, Adolfo Bioy Casares
and I took it up again to make a screenplay that film companies rejected enthusiastically and which would have been called
Los orilleros [Riverbank Men]. I thought, after such extensive
labors, that I had said good-bye to the story of the indifferent
duel; then this year, in Chivilcoy, I picked up a much better version that I hope is the true one, although both could be, since
destiny prefers to repeat forms, and what happened once happens often. Two mediocre stories and a film I believe to be good
came out of the deficient version; nothing can come out of the
second one, which is perfect and complete. Without adding
metaphors or scenery, I shall tell it as it was told to me. The
story, as they told me, took place in the district of Chivilcoy,
sometime in the 1870s. Wenceslao Suárez—the hero's name—
works as a rope braider and lives in an adobe hut. A man about
forty or fifty years old, he has a reputation for bravery, and it is
likely (given the facts of the story) that he once killed a man or
two, but these deaths, committed in honor, do not trouble his
conscience or sully his fame. One evening in this man's sedate
life, something unexpected happens; in the general store, he is
told that a letter for him has arrived. Don Wenceslao does not
know how to read; the bartender haltingly deciphers the ceremonious missive, which also does not seem to be handwritten
by the man who sent it. In the name of certain friends who

value dexterity and true composure, the stranger greets don Wenceslao, whose fame has crossed the Arroyo del Medio, and offers him the hospitality of his humble home in a town in the province of Santa Fe. Wenceslao Suárez dictates a reply to the bartender, thanking the stranger for his expression of friendship, and explains that he dare not leave his mother—who's well along in years—alone, but invites the other man to his simple abode in Chivilcoy, where he will be welcome to partake of a side of beef and a bottle of wine. Months pass, and a man on a horse harnessed and saddled in a manner unfamiliar to the area shows up at the general store and asks for Suárez's address. Suárez, who has come in to buy meat, overhears the question and tells him who he is; the stranger reminds him of the letters they wrote each other a while ago. Suárez is delighted that the other man has decided to come, and the two of them go off to a nearby field, where Suárez prepares the barbecue. They eat and drink and talk. About what? I suspect about bloodshed and barbarian matters, but with wary formality. They have eaten lunch, and the heavy afternoon heat hangs over the land when the stranger invites don Wenceslao to join him in a bit of knife play. To say no would mean dishonor. The two men practice and play at fighting at first, but Wenceslao soon realizes that the stranger intends to kill him. He finally understands the meaning of the ceremonious letter and regrets having eaten and drunk so much. He knows that he will tire before the other man, who is still young. Out of scorn or courtesy, the stranger proposes a short rest. Don Wenceslao accepts, and when they resume the duel, he lets the other man wound him in the left hand, around which he has rolled his poncho.[3] The knife cuts through his wrist, the hand hangs loose, as if dead. Suárez leaps backward,

---

3 Montaigne in his *Essays* (I, 49) speaks of this olden manner of combat with cape and sword, and cites a passage from Caesar: "*Sinistras sagis involvunt, gladiosque distringunt*" [They wrapped their cloaks around their left arms and drew their swords]. Lugones, in *El payador* [The Itinerant Singer], quotes an analogous motif in a sixteenth-century romance of Bernardo del Carpio: "*Revolviendo el manto al brazo, / La espada fuera a sacar*" [Wrapping the mantle round his arm / He would draw his sword].

lays his bloodied hand on the ground, steps on it with his boot, tears it off, fakes a blow to the stranger's chest, and with one thrust rips open his belly. Thus ends the story, save that in one version, the man from Santa Fe is left in the field, and in another (which steals from him the dignity of death) he returns to his province. In this last version, Suárez gives him first aid with the rum left over from lunch. . . .

In this feat of Manco [One Hand] Wenceslao—as Suárez is now known—certain mild or polite touches (his trade as rope maker, his scruples about leaving his mother alone, the two flowery letters, the conversation, the lunch) happily tone down or amplify the barbarous tale, giving it an epic or even chivalrous dimension that we do not find (unless we are determined to find it) in the drunken brawls of *Martín Fierro* or in the similar but paltry version about Juan Muraña and the Southside man. One feature common to both is, perhaps, significant. In both, the challenger is defeated. The reason may be the mere, deplorable necessity for the local champion to triumph, but also (and this is preferable) a tacit condemnation of provocation in these heroic fictions, or—this would be best of all—the dark and tragic conviction that man is always the maker of his own doom, like Ulysses in Canto XXVI of the *Inferno*. Emerson, who praised in Plutarch's biographies "a Stoicism not of the schools, but of the blood," would not have disdained this story.

We would seem to have, then, men who lived in utter poverty, gauchos and others from the banks of the River Plate and the Parana, creating, without realizing it, a religion that had its mythology and its martyrs—the hard and blind religion of courage, of being ready to kill and to die. A religion as old as the world, but rediscovered in the American republics and lived by herders, stockyard workers, drovers, outlaws, and hoodlums whose music was the *estilos*, the *milongas*, the first tangos. I have written that this religion is an age-old cult; in a twelfth-century saga we read:

"Tell me thy faith," said the count.
"I believe in my own strength," said Sigmund.

Wenceslao Suárez and his anonymous contender, and others whom mythology has forgotten or has embodied in these two, doubtless professed such a manly faith, which in all likelihood was not vanity but an awareness that God may be found in any man.

[1955]   *[SJL]*

MISCELLANY

(1931–51)

OUR INABILITIES

This fractional note on the most apparently grievous character-istics of the Argentine requires a prior limitation. Its subject is the Argentine of the cities, the mysterious, everyday specimen who venerates the lofty splendor of the meat-packing and cattle-auctioning professions; who travels by bus, which he con-siders a lethal weapon; who despises the United States and cel-ebrates the fact that Buenos Aires stands shoulder to shoulder with Chicago, homicidally speaking; who rejects the possibility of a Russian who is uncircumcised or hairless; who intuits a secret relationship between perverse or nonexistent virility and blond tobacco; who lovingly exercises the digital pantomime of the pseudo-serious; who on certain celebratory evenings engorges portions of digestive or evacuative or genetic appa-ratuses in traditional restaurants of recent apparition, called "grills"; who simultaneously prides himself on our "Latin ideal-ism" and our "Buenos Aires shrewdness"; who naively believes only in shrewdness. I will not concern myself with the *criollo*: a *maté*-driven conversationalist and storyteller who is without racial obligations. The present-day *criollo*—the one from the province of Buenos Aires, at least—is a linguistic variation, a set of behaviors that is exercised at times to discomfort, at other times to please. An example is the aging gaucho, whose irony and pride represent a subtle form of servility, for they confirm his popular image. . . . The *criollo*, I think, needs to be studied in those regions where a foreign audience has not stylized or falsified him—for example, in Uruguay's northern provinces. I return, then, to our everyday Argentine. I will not inquire into his complete definition, but rather his most apparent traits.

The first is the poverty of his imagination. For the typical Argentine, anything irregular is monstrous—and therefore ridiculous. The dissident who lets his beard grow in an age of the clean-shaven, or is crowned by a top hat in a neighborhood of homburgs, is a wonder and an impossibility and a scandal for those who see him. In the music halls, the familiar types of the Spaniard from Galicia and the Italian immigrant are mere parodical opposites of the *criollo*. They are not evil—which would give them a kind of dignity—they are momentary objects of laughter, mere nobodies. They uselessly gesticulate: even the fundamental seriousness of death is denied them. The fantasy corresponds with crude precision to our false securities. *This*, for us, is the foreigner: an unforgivable, always mistaken, largely unreal creature. The ineptitude of our actors helps. Lately, after Buenos Aires's eleven good lads were mistreated by Montevideo's eleven bad lads, the worst foreigner of all has become the Uruguayan. When one lies to oneself and insists on irreconcilable differences with faceless outsiders, what becomes of the real people? It is impossible to admit them as responsible members of the world. The failure of that intense film *Hallelujah* to reach the audiences of this country—or rather, the failure of the audiences of this country to reach *Hallelujah*—was the inevitable combination of that incapacity (exacerbated in this case because the subjects were black) with another, no less deplorable or symptomatic: the incapacity to accept true fervor without mockery. This mortal and comfortable negligence of everything in the world that is not Argentine is a pompous self-valorization of the place our country occupies among the other nations. A few months ago, after the logical outcome of a gubernatorial election, people began talking about "Russian gold" as if the internal politics of a province of this faded republic would be even perceptible in Moscow, let alone of importance. A strong megalomaniacal will permits these legends. Our complete lack of curiosity is effusively displayed in all our graphic magazines, which are as ignorant of the five continents and the seven seas as they are solicitous toward the wealthy summer vacationers in Mar del Plata, the objects of their vile ardor, their veneration, and their vigilance. Not only is the general vision impoverished here, but also the domestic one. The native's map of Buenos Aires is well known: downtown, the Barrio Norte (aseptically omitting its tenements), the Boca del Riachuelo, and Belgrano. The rest is an inconvenient Cimmeria, a useless conjectural stop for the bus on its return trip to the outskirts.

The other trait I shall attempt to demonstrate is the unrestrainable delight in failure. In the movie houses of this city, crushed hopes are applauded in the merry balconies as if they were comic. The same occurs when there is a fight scene: the loser's humiliation is far more interesting than the winner's happiness. In one of von Sternberg's heroic films, the tall gangster Bull Weed staggers over the fallen streamers at the ruinous end of a party to kill his drunken rival, who, seeing the awkward but steadfast approach of Weed, runs for his life. The outbursts of laughter celebrating his terror remind us what hemisphere we are in. At the poorer movie houses, any hint of aggression is enough to excite the public. This ever-ready resentment had its joyous articulation in the imperative "*¡sufra!*" [suffer!], which has lately been retired from our lips, but not from our hearts. The interjection "*¡toma!*" [take it!] is also significant; it is used by Argentine women to crown any enumeration of splendors—for example, the opulent stages of a summer holiday—as if delights were measured by the envious irritation they produce. (We note, in passing, that the most sincere compliment in Spanish is "enviable.") Another illustration of the Buenos Airean's facility for hate is the considerable number of anonymous messages, among which we must now include the new auditory anonymity: the offensive telephone call, an invulnerable broadcast of insults. I do not know if this impersonal and modest literary genre is an Argentine invention, but it is practiced here often and enthusiastically. There are virtuosos in this capital who season the indecency of their vocatives with the studious untimeliness of the hour. Nor do our fellow citizens often forget that great speed may be a form of good breeding and that the insults shouted at pedestrians from a whizzing car maintain a general impunity. It is true that the recipient is equally anonymous and the brief spectacle of his rage grows smaller until it vanishes, but it is always a relief to insult. I will add another curious example: sodomy. In all the countries of the world, an indivisible reprobation falls back upon the two parties of that unimaginable contact. "Both of them have committed an abomination . . . their blood shall be upon them," says Leviticus. Not among the tough guys of Buenos Aires, who proclaim a kind of veneration for the active partner—because he took advantage of his companion. I submit this fecal dialectic to the apologists for "shrewdness," the wisecrack, and the backbite, which cover over so much hell.

A poverty of imagination and resentment define our place in death. The former is vouched for by a generalizing article by Unamuno on "The Imagination in Cochabamba"; the latter by the incomparable spectacle of a conservative government that is forcing the entire republic into socialism, merely to annoy and depress a centrist party.

I have been an Argentine for many generations and express these complaints with no joy.

[1931]   [EW]

I, A JEW

Like the Druzes, like the moon, like death, like next week, the distant past is one of those things that can enrich ignorance. It is infinitely malleable and agreeable, far more obliging than the future and far less demanding of our efforts. It is the famous season favored by all mythologies.

Who has not, at one time or another, played with thoughts of his ancestors, with the prehistory of his flesh and blood? I have done so many times, and many times it has not displeased me to think of myself as Jewish. It is an idle hypothesis, a frugal and sedentary adventure that harms no one, not even the name of Israel, as my Judaism is wordless, like the songs of Mendelssohn. The magazine *Crisol* [Crucible], in its issue of January 30, has decided to gratify this retrospective hope; it speaks of my "Jewish ancestry, maliciously hidden" (the participle and the adverb amaze and delight me).

Borges Acevedo is my name. Ramos Mejía, in a note to the fifth chapter of *Rosas and His Times*, lists the family names in Buenos Aires at that time in order to demonstrate that all, or almost all, "came from Judeo-Portuguese stock." "Acevedo" is included in the list: the only supporting evidence for my Jewish pretensions until this confirmation in *Crisol*. Nevertheless, Captain Honorio Acevedo undertook a detailed investigation that I cannot ignore. His study notes that the first Acevedo to disembark on this land was the Catalan don Pedro de Azevedo in 1728: landholder, settler of "Pago de Los Arroyos," father and grandfather of cattle ranchers in that province, a notable who figures in the annals of the parish of Santa Fe and in the documents of the history of the viceroyalty—an ancestor, in short, irreparably Spanish.

Two hundred years and I can't find the Israelite; two hundred years and my ancestor still eludes me.

I am grateful for the stimulus provided by *Crisol*, but hope is dimming that I will ever be able to discover my link to the Table of the Breads and the Sea of Bronze; to Heine, Gleizer, and the ten Sefiroth; to Ecclesiastes and Chaplin.

Statistically, the Hebrews were few. What would we think of someone in the year 4000 who uncovers people from San Juan Province everywhere? Our inquisitors seek out Hebrews, but never Phoenicians, Garamantes, Scythians, Babylonians, Persians, Egyptians, Huns, Vandals, Ostrogoths, Ethiopians, Illyrians, Paphlagonians, Sarmatians, Medes, Ottomans, Berbers, Britons, Libyans, Cyclopes, or Lapiths. The nights of Alexandria, of Babylon, of Carthage, of Memphis, never succeeded in engendering a single grandfather; it was only to the tribes of the bituminous Dead Sea that this gift was granted.

[1934]   [EW]

BORGES'S PROLOGUE TO THE GERMAN EDITION OF ENRIQUE AMORIM'S
La carreta

The principal traits of *literatura gauchesca*, from either bank of the Río de la Plata, have been proudly enumerated more than once: its rustic vigor, its Homeric affinities, its pardonable or (more accurately) admirable incorrectness, its authenticity. Having admitted (and even venerated) those extremely pleasing traits, I'd dare to add (in low tones) another, no less indubitable than unspoken: the exclusively urban origin of all that sylvan literature.

Of course, it was the work of city dwellers who became intimate with the country and its gauchos, so it's unfair to accuse it of factual errors, of mere mistakes of fact. Its more habitual error is of another order: I'm referring to its bad sentimental habits. The writer from Buenos Aires or Montevideo who talks about gauchos has a propensity for myth, voluntarily or involuntarily. More than a hundred years of earlier literature weigh on that writer.

The study of literature is curious. Jokes, vacillations, and parodies prefigure the demigod. The Uruguayan Hidalgo, father of the first gaucho writers, was ignorant of the fact that their generation was divine and moved them with complete familiarity. The same is true of Ascasubi as well in the felicitous and bellicose cantos of *Paulino Lucero*.

There is joy in those cantos, and jokes, but never nostalgia, which is why Buenos Aires has forgotten and omitted them completely, to the advantage of the same author's garrulous and senile "Santos Vega": an impenetrable succession of thirteen thousand verses woven in the disconsolate Paris of 1871. That languid chronicle—the product of an old Argentine military man suffering nostalgia for his homeland and for his years of brio—inaugurated the myth of the gaucho. In the preface to the first edition, Ascasubi declared his apologetic intention: "Finally [he says], since I think I'm not mistaken when I think there is no character better than the country people of our lands, I've always tried to emphasize the good aspects that usually adorn the character of the gaucho."

Those words are from 1872. That same year, Hernández published in Buenos Aires the first section of the founding text of *literatura gauchesca*: *Martín Fierro*. Martín Fierro is a gaucho gone bad: The army is guilty of his perdition and sad fate. The popularity achieved by *Martín Fierro* created the need for other gauchos, no less oppressed by the law and no less heroic. Eduardo Gutiérrez, a writer unjustly forgotten, supplied them in infinite number. His method and his intent are both mythological. He attempted, like all authors of myths, to repeat a reality. He composed biographies of bad gauchos in order to justify them. One day, fed up, he repented. He wrote *Hormiga Negra*, a book of total disillusionment. Buenos Aires perused it coldly; his publishers did not reprint it. . . .

Around 1913, Leopoldo Lugones, in the packed Odeon Theater, read his tumultuous apology for the *Martín Fierro* and for the gaucho as well. Even so, the apotheosis was still missing. Ricardo Güiraldes attempted it and brought it to a conclusion in *Don Segundo Sombra*. The entire book is governed by memory, by reverent and nostalgic memory. In *Don Segundo*, the risk, hardship, and austerity the gaucho endures are rendered gigantic by memory. The explanation is easy. Güiraldes works with the past of the province of Buenos Aires, a province where immigration, farming, and railroads profoundly alter the gaucho as a type.

Enrique Amorim works with the present. The material for his novels is the Uruguayan countryside today: the hard countryside of the north, a land of taciturn gauchos, red bulls, hell-for-leather smugglers, narrow roads where the wind wears itself out, tall carts that carry a fatigue miles long. A land of *estancias* that stand alone like ships at sea and where the incessant solitude oppresses men.

Enrique Amorim does not write in the service of a myth, nor does he write against one. He is interested, as all authentic novelists are, in people, facts, motives, and not general symbols. (Which does not mean that his characters cannot be interpreted in symbolic terms; reality itself can be.) In Amorim's pages, the men and deeds of the countryside appear without reverence and without disdain, entirely natural. I know that this book will be a *gevaltiges Erlebnis* for the German reader.[1]

[1937]   [AMA]

---

1 This prologue was published as "A Novel by Amorim in German" with the following statement:

> The most recent mail from Europe brought with it the first copies of *La carreta*, a novel by our collaborator Enrique Amorim, translated into German and published by Holle in Berlin. This is a significant event for the literature of the Río de la Plata region, not exactly for what it adds to the wider reputation of the author but for what it implies as an opinion of a literature so distant from known European preferences, especially those of Germany. In the care and scrupulousness of this translation of *La carreta*, we see the intelligence with which its content was valorized, a value augmented in some degree by a prologue by Jorge Luis Borges, whose translation we reproduce here.

[AMA]

DEFINITION OF A
GERMANOPHILE

The implacable detractors of etymology argue that the origins of words do not instruct us in what they now mean; its defenders could reply that origins always instruct us in what words no longer mean. They demonstrate, for example, that pontiffs are not builders of bridges; that miniatures are not painted with minium; that crystal is not composed of ice; that the leopard is not a cross between a panther and a lion; that a candidate need not be robed in white; that sarcophagi are not the opposite of vegetarians; that alligators are not lizards; that rubrics are not red; that the discoverer of America was not Amerigo Vespucci; and that Germanophiles are not devotees of Germany.

This last is neither incorrect, nor even an exaggeration. I have been naive enough to talk with many Argentine Germanophiles; I have tried to speak of Germany and the German things that are imperishable; I have mentioned Hölderlin, Luther, Schopenhauer, and Leibniz; I have discovered that my "Germanophile" interlocutor could barely identify those names and preferred to discuss a more or less Antarctic archipelago that the English discovered in 1592 and whose relation to Germany I have yet to perceive.

Total ignorance of things Germanic does not, however, exhaust the definition of our Germanophiles. There are other unique characteristics that are, perhaps, equally essential. Among them: the Germanophile is greatly distressed that the railroad companies of a certain South American republic have English stockholders. He is also troubled by the hardships of the South African war of 1902. He is also anti-Semitic, and wishes to expel from our country a Slavo-Germanic community in which names of German origin predominate (Rosenblatt, Gruenberg, Nierenstein, Lilienthal) and which speaks a German dialect: Yiddish.

One might infer from this that the Germanophile is actually an Anglophobe. He is perfectly ignorant of Germany, and reserves his enthusiasm for any country at war with England. We shall see that such is the truth, but not the whole truth, nor even its most significant part. To demonstrate this I will reconstruct, reducing it to its essentials, a conversation I have had with many Germanophiles—something in which I swear never to involve myself again, for the time granted to mortals is not infinite and the fruit of these discussions is vain.

Invariably, my interlocutor begins by condemning the Treaty of Versailles, imposed by sheer force on Germany in 1919. Invariably, I illustrate the inculpatory judgment with a text from Wells or Bernard Shaw, who, in the hour of victory, denounced that implacable document. The Germanophile never rejects this text. He proclaims that a victorious country must abjure oppression and vengeance. He proclaims it natural that Germany wanted to annul that outrage. I share his opinion. Afterward, immediately afterward, the inexplicable occurs. My prodigious interlocutor argues that the old injustice suffered by Germany authorizes it, in 1940, to destroy not only England and France (why not Italy?), but also Denmark, Holland, and Norway, who are all completely free of blame for that injustice. In 1919, Germany was badly treated by its enemies: that all-powerful reason now allows it to burn, raze, and conquer all the nations of Europe and perhaps the globe. . . . The reasoning is monstrous, as can be seen.

I timidly point out this monstrousness to my interlocutor. He laughs at my antiquated scruples and raises Jesuitical or Nietzschean arguments: the end justifies the means, necessity knows no law, there is no law other than the will of the strongest, the

Reich is strong, the air forces of the Reich have destroyed Coventry, etc. I mumble that I am resigned to passing from the morality of Jesus to that of Zarathustra or the Black Ant but that our rapid conversion then prohibits us from pitying Germany for the injustice it suffered in 1919. On that date which he does not want to forget, England and France were strong; there is no law other than the will of the strongest; therefore, those calumnied nations acted correctly in wanting to ruin Germany, and one cannot condemn them for anything other than having been indecisive (and even culpably merciful) in the execution of that plan. Disdaining these dry abstractions, my interlocutor begins or outlines a panegyric to Hitler: that providential man whose indefatigable discourses preach the extinction of all charlatans and demagogues, and whose incendiary bombs, unmitigated by verbose declarations of war, announce from the firmament the ruin of rapacious imperialism. Afterward, immediately afterward, a second wonder occurs. It is of a moral nature and almost unbelievable.

I always discover that my interlocutor idolizes Hitler, not in spite of the high-altitude bombs and the rumbling invasions, the machine guns, the accusations and lies, but because of those acts and instruments. He is delighted by evil and atrocity. The triumph of Germany does not matter to him; he wants the humiliation of England and a satisfying burning of London. He admires Hitler as he once admired his precursors in the criminal underworld of Chicago. The discussion becomes impossible because the offenses I ascribe to Hitler are, for him, wonders and virtues. The apologists of Amigas, Ramírez, Quiroga, Rosas, or Urquiza pardon or gloss over their crimes; the defender of Hitler derives a special pleasure from them. The Hitlerist is always a spiteful man, and a secret and sometimes public worshiper of criminal "vivacity" and cruelty. He is, thanks to a poverty of imagination, a man who believes that the future cannot be different from the present, and that Germany, till now victorious, cannot lose. He is the cunning man who longs to be on the winning side.

It is not entirely impossible that there could be some

justification for Adolf Hitler; I know there is none for the Germanophile.

[1940]   [EW]

1941

The notion of an atrocious conspiracy by Germany to conquer and oppress all the countries of the atlas is (I rush to admit) irrevocably banal. It seems an invention of Maurice Leblanc, of Mr. Phillips Oppenheim, or of Baldur von Schirach. Notoriously anachronistic, it has the unmistakable flavor of 1914. Symptomatic of a poor imagination, grandiosity, and crass make-believe, this deplorable German fable counts on the complicity of the oblique Japanese and the docile, untrustworthy Italians, a circumstance that makes it even more ridiculous. . . . Unfortunately, reality lacks literary scruples. All liberties are permitted, even a coincidence with Maurice Leblanc. As versatile as it is monotonous, reality lacks nothing, not even the purest indigence. Two centuries after the published ironies of Voltaire and Swift, our astonished eyes have seen the Eucharist Congress; men fulminated against by Juvenal rule the destinies of the world. That we are readers of Russell, Proust, and Henry James matters not; we are in the rudimentary world of the slave Aesop and cacophonic Marinetti. Ours is a paradoxical destiny.

Le vrai peut quelque fois n'être pas vraisemblable: the unbelievable, indisputable truth is that the directors of the Third Reich are procuring a universal empire, the conquest of the world. I will not enumerate the countries they have already attacked and plundered, not wishing this page to be infinite. Yesterday the Germanophiles swore that the maligned Hitler did not even dream of attacking this continent; now they justify and praise his latest hostility. They have applauded the invasion of Norway and Greece, the Soviet Republics and Holland; who knows what celebrations they will unleash the day our cities and shores are razed. It is childish to be impatient; Hitler's charity is ecumenical; in short (if the traitors and Jews don't disrupt him) we will enjoy all the benefits of torture, sodomy, rape, and mass executions. Do not our plains abound in *Lebensraum*, unlimited and precious matter? Someone, to frustrate our hopes, observes that we are very far away. My answer to him is that colonies are always far from the metropolis; the Belgian Congo is not on the borders of Belgium.

[*1941*]   [*SJL*]

OUR POOR INDIVIDUALISM

There is no end to the illusions of patriotism. In the first century of our era, Plutarch mocked those who declared that the Athenian moon is better than the Corinthian moon; Milton, in the seventeenth, observed that God is in the habit of revealing Himself first to His Englishmen; Fichte, at the beginning of the nineteenth, declared that to have character and to be German are obviously one and the same thing. Here in Argentina we are teeming with nationalists, driven, they claim, by the worthy or innocent resolve of promoting the best traits of the Argentine people. Yet they ignore the Argentine people; in their polemics they prefer to define them as a function of some external fact, the Spanish conquistadors, say, or an imaginary Catholic tradition, or "Saxon imperialism."

The Argentine, unlike the Americans of the North and almost all Europeans, does not identify with the State. This is attributable to the circumstance that the governments in this country tend to be awful, or to the general fact that the State is an inconceivable abstraction.[1] One thing is certain: the Argentine is an individual, not a citizen. Aphorisms such as Hegel's "The State is the reality of the moral idea" strike him as sinister jokes. Films made in Hollywood often hold up for admiration the case of a man (usually a journalist) who seeks out the friendship of a criminal in order to hand him over to the police; the

[1] The State is impersonal; the Argentine can only conceive of personal relations. Therefore, to him, robbing public funds is not a crime. I am noting a fact; I am not justifying or excusing it.

Argentine, for whom friendship is a passion and the police a mafia, feels that this "hero" is an incomprehensible swine. He feels with Don Quixote that "everybody hath sins of his own to answer for" and that "it is not seemly, that honest men should be the executioners of their fellow-creatures, on account of matters with which they have no concern" (*Quixote* I, XXII). More than once, confronted with the vain symmetries of the Spanish style, I have suspected that we are irredeemably different from Spain; these two lines from the *Quixote* have sufficed to convince me of my error; they seem to be the secret, tranquil symbol of our affinity. This is profoundly confirmed by a single night in Argentine literature: the desperate night when a sergeant in the rural police shouted that he was not going to consent to the crime of killing a brave man, and started fighting against his own soldiers alongside the fugitive Martín Fierro.

The world, for the European, is a cosmos in which each individual personally corresponds to the role he plays; for the Argentine, it is a chaos. The European and the North American consider that a book that has been awarded any kind of prize must be good; the Argentine allows for the possibility that the book might not be bad, despite the prize. In general, the Argentine does not believe in circumstances. He may be unaware of the fable that humanity always includes thirty-six just men— the Lamed Wufniks—who are unknown to one another, but who secretly sustain the universe; if he hears of it, it does not strike him as strange that these worthies are obscure and anonymous. . . . His popular hero is the lone man who quarrels with the group, either actually (Fierro, Moreira, the Black Ant), potentially, or in the past (Segundo Sombra). Other literatures do not record analogous events. Consider, for example, two great European writers: Kipling and Franz Kafka. At first glance, the two have nothing in common, but Kipling's subject is the defense of order, of an order (the road in *Kim*, the bridge in *The Bridge-Builders*, the Roman wall in *Puck of Pook's Hill*); Kafka's, the unbearable, tragic solitude of the individual who lacks even the lowliest place in the order of the universe.

It may be said that the traits I have pointed out are merely negative or anarchic; it may be added that they are not subject to political explanation. I shall venture to suggest the opposite. The most urgent problem of our time (already denounced with prophetic lucidity by the near-forgotten Spencer) is the gradual interference of the State in the acts of the individual, in the battle with this evil, whose names are communism and Nazism, Argentine individualism, though perhaps useless or harmful until now, will find its justification and its duties.

Without hope and with nostalgia, I think of the abstract possibility of a party that had some affinity with the Argentine people; a party that would promise (let us say) a strict minimum of government.

Nationalism seeks to captivate us with the vision of an infinitely tiresome State; this utopia, once established on earth, would have the providential virtue of making everyone yearn for, and finally build, its antithesis.

[1946]   [EA]

THE ARGENTINE WRITER
AND TRADITION

I would like to express and justify certain skeptical propositions concerning the problem of the Argentine writer and tradition. My skepticism is not related to the difficulty or impossibility of resolving the problem, but to its very existence. I think we are faced with a rhetorical theme, suitable for pathetic elaboration, rather than a true cerebral difficulty; it is, to my mind, an appearance, a simulacrum, a pseudo-problem.

Before examining it, I would like to consider its standard expressions and solutions. I will start with a solution that has become almost instinctive and presents itself without benefit of any rationale: the one which affirms that the Argentine literary tradition already exists in *gauchesco* poetry. Consequently, the lexicon, techniques, and subject matter of *gauchesco* poetry should enlighten the contemporary writer, and are a point of departure and perhaps an archetype. This is the most common solution, and for that reason I intend to examine it at some length.

It was proposed by Lugones in *El payador*; there we read that we Argentines possess a classic poem, *Martín Fierro*, and that this poem should be for us what the Homeric poems were for the Greeks. It seems difficult to contradict this opinion without detriment to *Martín Fierro*. I believe that *Martín Fierro* is the most lasting work we Argentines have written; I also believe, with equal intensity, that we cannot take *Martín Fierro* to be, as has sometimes been said, our Bible, our canonical book.

Ricardo Rojas, who has also recommended the canonization

of *Martín Fierro*, has written a page, in his *Historia de la literatura Argentina*, that appears to be almost a platitude, but is quite shrewd.

Rojas studies the poetry of the *gauchescos*—the poetry of Hidalgo, Ascasubi, Estanislao del Campo, and José Hernández—and finds its origins in the poetry of the rural improvisational singers known as *payadores*, that is, the spontaneous poetry of the gauchos themselves. He points out that the meter of this popular poetry is octosyllabic, the same meter used by the authors of *gauchesco* poetry, and he concludes by considering the poetry of the *gauchescos* to be a continuation or magnification of the poetry of the *payadores*.

I suspect that this claim is based on a serious mistake; we might also call it a clever mistake, for it is clear that Rojas, in order to give popular roots to the poetry of the *gauchescos*, which begins with Hidalgo and culminates with Hernández, presents it as a continuation or derivation of the poetry of the gauchos; therefore Bartolomé Hidalgo is not the Homer of this poetry, as Mitre said, but only a link in the sequence.

Ricardo Rojas makes a *payador* of Hidalgo; nevertheless, according to the same *Historia de la literatura Argentina*, this supposed *payador* began by composing lines of eleven syllables, a meter that is by its very nature barred to *payadores*, who do not perceive its harmony, just as Spanish readers did not perceive the harmony of the hendecasyllabic line when Garcilaso imported it from Italy.

There is, to my mind, a fundamental difference between the poetry of the gauchos and *gauchesco* poetry. One need only compare any collection of popular poetry with *Martín Fierro, Paulino Lucero*, or the *Fausto* to become aware of this difference, which exists equally in the lexicon and in the intent of the poets. The popular poets of the countryside and the outskirts of the city versify general themes: the pain of love and absence, the sorrow of love, and they do so in a lexicon that is equally general; the *gauchesco* poets, on the contrary, cultivate a deliberately popular language that the popular poets do not even attempt. I do not mean that the idiom of the popular poets is a correct Spanish, I mean that whatever may be incorrect in it results from ignorance. In the *gauchesco* poets, on the contrary, there is a quest for native words, a profusion of local color. The proof is this: a Colombian, a Mexican, or a Spaniard can immediately understand the poems of the *payadores*—the gauchos—but needs a glossary in order to reach even an approximate understanding of Estanislao del Campo or Ascasubi.

All of this can be abbreviated as follows: *gauchesco* poetry, which has produced—I hasten to repeat—admirable works, is as artificial as any other literary genre. The first *gauchesco* compositions, the ballads of Bartolomé Hidalgo, attempt to present themselves in accordance with the gaucho, as if spoken by gauchos, so that the reader will read them with a gaucho intonation. Nothing could be further from popular poetry. When they versify, the people—and I have observed this not only among the *payadores* of the countryside, but also in the neighborhoods of Buenos Aires—do so in the conviction that they are engaging in something important; therefore they instinctively reject popular words and seek out high-sounding words and turns of phrase. In all likelihood, *gauchesco* poetry has influenced the *payadores* by now, so that they, too, abound in Argentinisms, but initially this was not the case, and we have evidence of that (evidence no one has noted) in *Martín Fierro*.

Martín Fierro is written in a *gauchesco*-accented Spanish, and for a long while the poem does not allow us to forget that the person singing it is a gaucho; it abounds in comparisons taken from life in the grasslands; and yet there is a famous passage in which the author forgets this concern with local color and writes in a general Spanish, speaking not of vernacular subjects but of great, abstract subjects: time, space, the sea, the night. I am referring to the *payada*, the improvised musical face-off between Martín Fierro and El Moreno that occupies the end of the second part. It is as if Hernández himself had wished to demonstrate the difference between his *gauchesco* poetry and the genuine poetry of the gauchos. When the two gauchos, Fierro and El Moreno, start singing, they forget all *gauchesco* affectation and address philosophical issues. I have been able to corroborate this by listening to *payadores* in the surroundings of Buenos Aires; they reject the idea of versifying

in street slang, in *orillero* and *lunfardo*, and try to express themselves correctly. Of course they fail, but their aim is to make of
poetry something high, something distinguished, we might say
with a smile.

The idea that Argentine poetry must abound in Argentine
differential traits and in Argentine local color seems to me to be
a mistake. If we ask which book is more Argentine, *Martín
Fierro* or the sonnets in *La urna* by Enrique Banchs, there is no
reason to say that the former is more Argentine. It will be said
that in Banchs's *La urna* there are neither Argentine landscapes
nor Argentine topography nor Argentine botany nor Argentine
zoology; nevertheless, there are other specifically Argentine conditions in *La urna*.

I can recall two lines of *La urna* that seem to have been written expressly to prevent anyone from saying that this is an
Argentine book; the lines are:

> *El sol en los tejados*
> *y en las ventanas brilla. Ruiseñores*
> *quieren decir que están enamorados.*

[The sun glints on the tiled roofs / and on the windows. Nightingales / mean to say they are in love.]

A denunciation of "the sun glints on the tiled roofs and on the
windows" seems inevitable here. Enrique Banchs wrote these
lines in a house on the edge of Buenos Aires, and on the edges
of Buenos Aires there are no tiled roofs, there are flat, terrace
roofs; "nightingales mean to say they are in love"; the nightin-
gale is not so much a real bird as a bird of literature, of the
Greek and Germanic tradition. Nevertheless, I would maintain
that in the use of these conventional images, in these incongru-
ous tiled roofs and nightingales, although neither the architecture nor the ornithology is Argentine, there is the Argentine
reserve, the Argentine reticence; the fact that Banchs, in speaking of a great sorrow that overwhelmed him, of a woman who
left him and left the world empty for him, makes use of conventional, foreign imagery such as tiled roofs and nightingales, is

significant: significant of a reserve, wariness, and reticence that are Argentine, significant of the difficulty we have in confiding, in being intimate.

Furthermore, I do not know if it needs to be said that the idea that a literature must define itself by the differential traits of the country that produces it is a relatively new one, and the idea that writers must seek out subjects local to their countries is also new and arbitrary. Without going back any further, I think Racine would not have begun to understand anyone who would deny him his right to the title of French poet for having sought out Greek and Latin subjects. I think Shakespeare would have been astonished if anyone had tried to limit him to English subjects, and if anyone had told him that, as an Englishman, he had no right to write *Hamlet*, with its Scandinavian subject matter, or *Macbeth*, on a Scottish theme. The Argentine cult of local color is a recent European cult that nationalists should reject as a foreign import.

A few days ago, I discovered a curious confirmation of the way in which what is truly native can and often does dispense with local color; I found this confirmation in Gibbon's *Decline and Fall of the Roman Empire*. Gibbon observes that in the Arab book *par excellence*, the Koran, there are no camels; I believe that if there were ever any doubt as to the authenticity of the Koran, this lack of camels would suffice to prove that it is Arab. It was written by Mohammed, and Mohammed, as an Arab, had no reason to know that camels were particularly Arab; they were, for him, a part of reality, and he had no reason to single them out, while the first thing a forger, a tourist, or an Arab nationalist would do is bring on the camels, whole caravans of camels on every page; but Mohammed, as an Arab, was unconcerned; he knew he could be Arab without camels. I believe that we Argentines can be like Mohammed; we can believe in the possibility of being Argentine without abounding in local color.

Permit me to confide something, just a small thing. For many years, in books now fortunately forgotten, I tried to compose the flavor, the essence, of the outskirts of Buenos Aires; naturally I abounded in local words such as *cuchilleros, milonga, tapia*, and others, and in such manner I wrote those forgettable and forgotten books; then, about a year ago, I wrote a story called "Death and the Compass," which is a kind of nightmare, a nightmare in which elements of Buenos Aires appear, deformed by the horror of the nightmare; and in that story, when I think of the Paseo Colón, I call it Rue de Toulon; when I think of the *quintas* of Adrogué, I call them Triste-le-Roy; after the story was published, my friends told me that at last they had found the flavor of the outskirts of Buenos Aires in my writing. Precisely because I had not abandoned myself to the dream, I was able to achieve, after so many years, what I once sought in vain.

Now I wish to speak of a justly illustrious work that the nationalists often invoke. I refer to *Don Segundo Sombra* by Güiraldes. The nationalists tell us that *Don Segundo Sombra* is the characteristic national book; but if we compare *Don Segundo Sombra* to the works of the *gauchesco* tradition, the first things we note are differences. *Don Segundo Sombra* abounds in a type of metaphor that has nothing to do with the speech of the countryside and everything to do with the metaphors of the Montmartre salons of that period. As for the plot, the story, it is easy to discern the influence of Kipling's *Kim*, which is set in India and was, in its turn, written under the influence of Mark Twain's *Huckleberry Finn*, the epic of the Mississippi. In making this observation, I do not wish to devalue *Don Segundo Sombra*; on the contrary, I wish to emphasize that in order for us to have this book it was necessary for Güiraldes to recall the poetic technique of the French salons of his time, and the work of Kipling, which he had read many years before; which is to say that Kipling and Mark Twain and the metaphors of the French poets were necessary to this Argentine book, to this book which is, I repeat, no less Argentine for having accepted those influences.

I wish to note another contradiction: the nationalists pretend to venerate the capacities of the Argentine mind but wish to limit the poetic exercise of that mind to a few humble local themes, as if we Argentines could only speak of neighborhoods and ranches and not of the universe.

Let us pass on to another solution. It is said that there is a tradition of which we Argentine writers must avail ourselves, and that tradition is the literature of Spain. This second piece of advice is, of course, a bit less narrow than the first, but it also tends to restrict us; many objections can be made to it, but two will suffice. The first is this: Argentine history can unequivocally be defined as a desire to move away from Spain, as a willed distancing from Spain. The second objection is that, among us, the pleasure of Spanish literature, a pleasure I personally share in, is usually an acquired taste; I have often loaned French and English works to people without any particular literary erudition, and those books were enjoyed immediately, without effort. However, when I have suggested that my friends read Spanish books, I have found that these books were difficult for them to enjoy in the absence of special training; I therefore believe that the fact that certain illustrious Argentine writers write like Spaniards is not so much a testimony to some inherited capacity as it is evidence of Argentine versatility.

I now arrive at a third opinion on Argentine writers and tradition, one that I read not long ago and that greatly astonished me. This is the opinion that we Argentines are cut off from the past; that there has been some sort of rupture between ourselves and Europe. According to this singular point of view, we Argentines are as if in the first days of creation; our search for European subject matters and techniques is an illusion, an error; we must understand that we are essentially alone, and cannot play at being European.

This opinion strikes me as unfounded. I understand why many people accept it: such a declaration of our solitude, our perdition, and our primitive character has, like existentialism, the charms of poignancy. Many people may accept this opinion because, having done so, they will feel themselves to be alone, disconsolate, and in some way, interesting. Nevertheless, I have observed that in our country, precisely because it is a new country, there is a strong feeling for time. Everything that has happened in Europe, the dramatic events there in recent years, has resonated deeply here. The fact that a given individual was on the side of Franco or the Republic during the Spanish Civil War, or was on the side of the Nazis or the Allies, was in many cases the cause of very serious disputes and estrangements. This would not happen if we were detached from Europe. As for Argentine history, I think we all feel it deeply; and it is only natural that we should, because that history is very close to us, in chronology and in the blood; the names, the battles of the civil wars, the war of independence, all of it is, in time and in family traditions, quite near.

What is Argentine tradition? I believe that this question poses no problem and can easily be answered. I believe that our tradition is the whole of Western culture, and I also believe that we have a right to this tradition, a greater right than that which the inhabitants of one Western nation or another may have. Here I remember an essay by Thorstein Veblen, the North American sociologist, on the intellectual preeminence of Jews in Western culture. He wonders if this preeminence authorizes us to posit an innate Jewish superiority and answers that it does not; he says that Jews are prominent in Western culture because they act within that culture and at the same time do not feel bound to it by any special devotion; therefore, he says, it will always be easier for a Jew than for a non-Jew to make innovations in Western culture. We can say the same of the Irish in English culture. Where the Irish are concerned, we have no reason to suppose that the profusion of Irish names in British literature and philosophy is due to any social preeminence, because many of these illustrious Irishmen (Shaw, Berkeley, Swift) were the descendants of Englishmen, men with no Celtic blood; nevertheless, the fact of feeling themselves to be Irish, to be different, was enough to enable them to make innovations in English culture. I believe that Argentines, and South Americans in general, are in an analogous situation; we can take on all the European subjects, take them on without superstition and with an irreverence that can have, and already has had, fortunate consequences.

This does not mean that all Argentine experiments are equally felicitous; I believe that this problem of the Argentine and tradition is simply a contemporary and fleeting version of the eternal problem of determinism. If I am going to touch this table with one of my hands, and I ask myself: "Will I touch it with the left hand or the right?" and I touch it with the right hand, the determinists will say that I could not have done otherwise and that the whole prior history of the universe forced me to touch the table with my right hand, and that touching it with my left hand would have been a miracle. Yet if I had touched it with my left hand, they would have told me the same thing: that I was forced to touch it with that hand. The same occurs with literary subjects and techniques. Everything we Argentine writers do felicitously will belong to Argentine tradition, in the same way that the use of Italian subjects belongs to the tradition of England through the work of Chaucer and Shakespeare.

I believe, moreover, that all the foregoing discussions of the aims of literary creation are based on the error of supposing that intentions and plans matter much. Take, for example, the case of Kipling: Kipling dedicated his life to writing in accordance with a given set of political ideals, he wanted to make his work a tool for propaganda, and nevertheless, at the end of his life he had to confess that the true essence of a writer's work is usually unknown by that writer; and he remembered the case of Swift, who while writing *Gulliver's Travels* wanted to raise an indictment against mankind and instead left behind a children's book. Plato said that poets are the amanuenses of a god who moves them against their will, against their intentions, as the magnet moves a series of iron rings.

Therefore I repeat that we must not be afraid; we must believe that the universe is our birthright and try out every subject; we cannot confine ourselves to what is Argentine in order to be Argentine because either it is our inevitable destiny to be Argentine, in which case we will be Argentine whatever we do, or being Argentine is a mere affectation, a mask.

I believe that if we lose ourselves in the voluntary dream called artistic creation, we will be Argentine and we will be, as well, good or adequate writers.

[1951]   [EA]

THE SOUTH

The man that stepped off the boat in Buenos Aires in 1871 was a minister of the Evangelical Church; his name was Johannes Dahlmann. By 1939, one of his grandsons, Juan Dahlmann, was secretary of a municipal library on Calle Córdoba and considered himself profoundly Argentine. His maternal grandfather had been Francisco Flores, of the 2nd Infantry of the Line, who died on the border of Buenos Aires from a spear wielded by the Indians under Catriel. In the contrary pulls from his two lineages, Juan Dahlmann (perhaps impelled by his Germanic blood) chose that of his romantic ancestor, or that of a romantic death. That slightly willful but never ostentatious "Argentinization" drew sustenance from an old sword, a locket containing the daguerreotype of a bearded, inexpressive man, the joy and courage of certain melodies, the habit of certain verses in *Martín Fierro*, the passing years, a certain lack of spiritedness, and solitude. At the price of some self-denial, Dahlmann had managed to save the shell of a large country house in the South that had once belonged to the Flores family; one of the touchstones of his memory was the image of the eucalyptus trees and the long pink-colored house that had once been scarlet. His work, and perhaps his indolence, held him in the city. Summer after summer he contented himself with the abstract idea of possession and with the certainty that his house was waiting for him, at a precise place on the flatlands. In late February, 1939, something happened to him.

Though blind to guilt, fate can be merciless with the slightest distractions. That afternoon Dahlmann had come upon a copy (from which some pages were missing) of Weil's *Arabian Nights*;

eager to examine his find, he did not wait for the elevator—he hurriedly took the stairs. Something in the dimness brushed his forehead—a bat? a bird? On the face of the woman who opened the door to him, he saw an expression of horror, and the hand he passed over his forehead came back red with blood. His brow had caught the edge of a recently painted casement window that somebody had forgotten to close. Dahlmann managed to sleep, but by the early hours of morning he was awake, and from that time on, the flavor of all things was monstrous to him. Fever wore him away, and illustrations from the *Arabian Nights* began to illuminate nightmares. Friends and members of his family would visit him and with exaggerated smiles tell him how well he looked. Dahlmann, in a kind of feeble stupor, would hear their words, and it would amaze him that they couldn't see he was in hell. Eight days passed, like eight hundred years. One afternoon, his usual physician appeared with a new man, and they drove Dahlmann to a sanatorium on Calle Ecuador; he needed to have an X-ray. Sitting in the cab they had hired to drive them, Dahlmann reflected that he might, at last, in a room that was not his own, be able to sleep. He felt happy, he felt like talking, but the moment they arrived, his clothes were stripped from him, his head was shaved, he was strapped with metal bands to a table, he was blinded and dizzied with bright lights, his heart and lungs were listened to, and a man in a surgical mask stuck a needle in his arm. He awoke nauseated, bandaged, in a cell much like the bottom of a well, and in the days and nights that followed, he realized that until then he had been only somewhere on the outskirts of hell. Ice left but the slightest trace of coolness in his mouth. During these days, Dahlmann hated every inch of himself; he hated his identity, his bodily needs, his humiliation, the beard that prickled his face. He stoically suffered the treatments administered to him, which were quite painful, but when the surgeon told him he'd been on the verge of death from septicemia, Dahlmann, suddenly self-pitying, broke down and cried. The physical miseries, the unending anticipation of bad nights had not allowed him to think about anything as abstract as death. The next day, the surgeon told him he was coming right along, and that he'd soon be able to go out to the country house to convalesce. Incredibly, the promised day arrived.

Reality is partial to symmetries and slight anachronisms; Dahlmann had come to the sanatorium in a cab, and it was a cab that took him to the station at Plaza Constitución. The first cool breath of autumn, after the oppression of the summer, was like a natural symbol of his life brought back from fever and the brink of death. The city, at that seven o'clock in the morning, had not lost that look of a ramshackle old house that cities take on at night; the streets were like long porches and corridors, the plazas like interior courtyards. After his long stay in hospital, Dahlmann took it all in with delight and a touch of vertigo; a few seconds before his eyes registered them, he would recall the corners, the marquees, the modest variety of Buenos Aires. In the yellow light of the new day, it all came back to him.

Everyone knows that the South begins on the other side of Avenida Rivadavia. Dahlmann had often said that that was no mere saying, that by crossing Rivadavia one entered an older and more stable world. From the cab, he sought among the new buildings the window barred with wrought iron, the door knocker, the arch of a doorway, the long entryway, the almost-secret courtyard.

In the grand hall of the station he saw that he had thirty minutes before his train left. He suddenly remembered that there was a café on Calle Brasil (a few yards from Yrigoyen's house) where there was a huge cat that would let people pet it, like some disdainful deity. He went in. There was the cat, asleep. He ordered a cup of coffee, slowly spooned sugar into it, tasted it (a pleasure that had been forbidden him in the clinic), and thought, while he stroked the cat's black fur, that this contact was illusory, that he and the cat were separated as though by a pane of glass, because man lives in time, in successiveness, while the magical animal lives in the present, in the eternity of the instant.

The train, stretching along the next-to-last platform, was waiting. Dahlmann walked through the cars until he came to one that was almost empty. He lifted his bag onto the luggage rack; when the train pulled out, he opened his bag and after a slight hesitation took from it the first volume of *The Arabian Nights*. To travel with this book so closely linked to the history of his torment was an affirmation that the torment was past, and was a joyous, secret challenge to the frustrated forces of evil.

On both sides of the train, the city unraveled into suburbs; that sight, and later the sight of lawns and large country homes, led Dahlmann to put aside his reading. The truth is, Dahlmann read very little; the lodestone mountain and the genie sworn to kill the man who released him from the bottle were, as anyone will admit, wondrous things, but not much more wondrous than this morning and the fact of being. Happiness distracted him from Scheherazade and her superfluous miracles; Dahlmann closed the book and allowed himself simply to live.

Lunch (with bouillon served in bowls of shining metal, as in the now-distant summers of his childhood) was another quiet, savored pleasure.

Tomorrow I will wake up at my ranch, he thought, and it was as though he were two men at once: the man gliding along through the autumn day and the geography of his native land, and the other man, imprisoned in a sanatorium and subjected to methodical attentions. He saw unplastered brick houses, long and angular, infinitely watching the trains go by; he saw horsemen on the clod-strewn roads; he saw ditches and lakes and pastures; he saw long glowing clouds that seemed made of marble, and all these things were fortuitous, like some dream of the flat prairies. He also thought he recognized trees and crops that he couldn't have told one the name of—his direct knowledge of the country was considerably inferior to his nostalgic, literary knowledge.

From time to time he nodded off, and in his dreams there was the rushing momentum of the train. Now the unbearable white sun of midday was the yellow sun that comes before nightfall and that soon would turn to red. The car was different now, too; it was not the same car that had pulled out of the station in Buenos Aires—the plains and the hours had penetrated and transfigured it. Outside, the moving shadow of the train stretched

out toward the horizon. The elemental earth was not disturbed
by settlements or any other signs of humanity. All was vast, but
at the same time intimate and somehow secret. In all the im-
mense countryside, there would sometimes be nothing but a
bull. The solitude was perfect, if perhaps hostile, and Dahlmann
almost suspected that he was traveling not only into the South
but into the past. From that fantastic conjecture he was distracted by the conductor, who seeing Dahlmann's ticket informed
him that the train would not be leaving him at the usual station,
but at a different one, a little before it, that Dahlmann barely
knew. (The man added an explanation that Dahlmann didn't try
to understand, didn't even listen to, because the mechanics of it
didn't matter.)

The train came to its laborious halt in virtually the middle of
the countryside. The station sat on the other side of the tracks,
and was hardly more than a covered platform. They had no
vehicle there, but the stationmaster figured Dahlmann might be
able to find one at a general store he directed him to—ten or
twelve blocks away.

Dahlmann accepted the walk as a small adventure. The sun
had sunk below the horizon now, but one final splendor brought
a glory to the living yet silent plains before they were blotted
out by night. Less to keep from tiring himself than to make
those things last, Dahlmann walked slowly, inhaling with grave
happiness the smell of clover.

The store had once been bright red, but the years had tem-
pered its violent color (to its advantage). There was something
in its sorry architecture that reminded Dahlmann of a steel en-
graving, perhaps from an old edition of *Paul et Virginie*. There
were several horses tied to the rail in front. Inside, Dahlmann
thought he recognized the owner; then he realized that he'd
been fooled by the man's resemblance to one of the employees
at the sanatorium. When the man heard Dahlmann's story, he
said he'd have the calash harnessed up; to add yet another event
to that day, and to pass the time, Dahlmann decided to eat there
in the country store.

At one table some rough-looking young men were noisily

eating and drinking; at first Dahlmann didn't pay much attention. On the floor, curled against the bar, lay an old man, as
motionless as an object. The many years had worn him away
and polished him, as a stone is worn smooth by running water
or a saying is polished by generations of humankind. He was
small, dark, and dried up, and he seemed to be outside time, in
a sort of eternity. Dahlmann was warmed by the rightness of
the man's hairband, the baize poncho he wore, his gaucho trousers, and the boots made out of the skin of a horse's leg, and he
said to himself, recalling futile arguments with people from dis-
tricts in the North, or from Entre Ríos, that only in the South
did gauchos like that exist anymore.

Dahlmann made himself comfortable near the window. Little
by little, darkness was enveloping the countryside, but the smells
and sounds of the plains still floated in through the thick iron
grate at the window. The storekeeper brought him sardines and
then roast meat; Dahlmann washed them down with more than
one glass of red wine. Idly, he savored the harsh bouquet of the
wine and let his gaze wander over the store, which by now had
turned a little sleepy. The kerosene lantern hung from one of the
beams. There were three customers at the other table: two
looked like laborers; the other, with coarse, Indian-like features,
sat drinking with his wide-brimmed hat on. Dahlmann suddenly felt something lightly brush his face. Next to the tumbler
of cloudy glass, on one of the stripes in the tablecloth, lay a
little ball of wadded bread. That was all, but somebody had
thrown it at him.

The drinkers at the other table seemed unaware of his presence.
Dahlmann, puzzled, decided that nothing had happened, and he
opened the volume of *The Arabian Nights*, as though to block
out reality. Another wad of bread hit him a few minutes later, and
this time the laborers laughed. Dahlmann told himself he wasn't
scared, but that it would be madness for him, a sick man, to be
dragged by strangers into some chaotic bar fight. He made up his
mind to leave; he was already on his feet when the storekeeper
came over and urged him, his voice alarmed: "Sr. Dahlmann,
ignore those boys over there—they're just feeling their oats."

Dahlmann did not find it strange that the storekeeper should know his name by now, but he sensed that the man's conciliatory words actually made the situation worse. Before, the men's provocation had been directed at an accidental face, almost at nobody; now it was aimed at him, at his name, and the men at the other table would know that name. Dahlmann brushed the storekeeper aside, faced the laborers, and asked them what their problem was.

The young thug with the Indian-looking face stood up, stumbling as he did so. At one pace from Dahlmann, he shouted insults at him, as though he were far away. He was playacting, exaggerating his drunkenness, and the exaggeration produced an impression both fierce and mocking. Amid curses and obscenities, the man threw a long knife into the air, followed it with his eyes, caught it, and challenged Dahlmann to fight. The storekeeper's voice shook as he objected that Dahlmann was unarmed. At that point, something unforeseeable happened.

From out of a corner, the motionless old gaucho in whom Dahlmann had seen a symbol of the South (the South that belonged to him) tossed him a naked dagger—it came to rest at Dahlmann's feet. It was as though the South itself had decided that Dahlmann should accept the challenge. Dahlmann bent to pick up the dagger, and as he did he sensed two things: first, that that virtually instinctive action committed him to fight, and second, that in his clumsy hand the weapon would serve less to defend him than to justify the other man's killing him. He had toyed with a knife now and then, as all men did, but his knowledge of knife fighting went no further than a vague recollection that thrusts should be aimed upward, and with the blade facing inward. *They'd never have allowed this sort of thing to happen in the sanatorium*, he thought.

"Enough stalling," the other man said. "Let's go outside."

They went outside, and while there was no hope in Dahlmann, there was no fear, either. As he crossed the threshold, he felt that on that first night in the sanatorium, when they'd stuck that needle in him, dying in a knife fight under the open sky, grappling with his adversary, would have been a liberation, a joy, and a fiesta. He sensed that had he been able to choose or dream his death that night, this is the death he would have dreamed or chosen.

Dahlmann firmly grips the knife, which he may have no idea how to manage, and steps out into the plains.

[1953]   [AH]

Glossary

Almafuerte (Pedro Bonifacio Palacios [1854–1917]). Like Evaristo Carriego, a minor, local, Buenos Aires poet dear to Borges's heart. The title of this posthumous volume summarizes Almafuerte's themes: *Milongas clásicas, sonetos medicinales, y Dios te salve* [Classical *milongas*, Medicinal Sonnets, and God Save You] (1919).

Álvarez, José Sixto (1858–1903). Argentine author who wrote under the name Fray Mocho. Depicted local scenes and customs. Founded the magazine *Caras y caretas*.

Amorim, Enrique (1900–1960). A Uruguayan landowner and member, in 1947, of the Uruguayan Communist Party, Amorim wrote about Uruguayan rural life. His novel *La carreta: Novela de quitanderas y vagabundos* [The Cart: Novel About Itinerant Prostitutes and Slackers] (1929) is about prostitution in northern Uruguay.

Arlt, Roberto (1900–1942). Argentine writer and journalist. His expressionistic novel in two volumes, *Los siete locos* [*The Seven Madmen*] (1929) and its sequel, *Los lanzallamas* [The Flamethrowers] (1931), uses *lunfardo* to enhance its construction of a hallucinated Buenos Aires.

Arrabal. A low-class section or neighborhood. The term is synonymous with *suburbio* or *orillas*.

Ascasubi, Hilario (1807–1875). A veteran of the Argentine civil wars and an *unitario*, Ascasubi is the author of *Aniceto el Gallo* (1853) and, more importantly, another work in gaucho style: *Santos Vega, o los mellizos de la Flor* [Santos Vega, or the Twins from La Flor Ranch] (1851). Eduardo Gutiérrez and Rafael Obligado also base works on the life of Santos Vega. By 1931, Borges had changed his mind about Ascasubi and published an article in the first issue of *Sur* stating his new point of view. That article reappears in his essay collection *Discusión*, as he says in the prologue: "'Colonel Ascasubi' [the new essay] nullifies and rejects another article on the same writer that I published many years ago."

Azotea. In traditional Spanish American architecture, a flat terrace, the roof of a one- or two-story structure, overlooking the patio of a house. Mediterranean in origin.

Bajo. A Buenos Aires neighborhood, the zone where the city formerly met the Río de la Plata.

Banchs, Enrique (1888–1968). An Argentine poet who stopped publishing after his 1911 collection of sonnets, *La urna* [The Urn].

Bandoneones. A concertinalike instrument invented by Heinrich Band (1821–1860), an essential part of an *orquesta típica* playing tangos.

Bernárdez, Francisco Luis (1900–1978). Argentine poet and lifelong friend of Borges.

Boca del Riachuelo. Also known as the Boca neighborhood in southeastern Buenos Aires. A lower-class neighborhood heavily Italian (Genoese), its name comes from the place where the La Matanza River (called El Riachuelo or Little River) enters the Plata. Home to the Boca Juniors football club.

Boedo-Florida. In 1924, a socialist writer, Roberto Mariani, published an article in the avant-garde magazine *Martín Fierro* accusing the magazine's contributors of being Francophile and not truly in touch with the people. Writers on the left came to be associated with Boedo, a street in a working-class Buenos Aires neighborhood, where their magazine, *Extrema izquierda* [Extreme Left] was published. The cosmopolitan writers became linked to another street, Florida, where the café they used as a meeting place, the Richmond, was located. A tempest in a teacup, the opposition rendered unity among *criollo* writers impossible. Put off by the pseudopolemic, Borges published "La inútil discusión de Boedo y Florida" [The Useless Argument About Boedo and Florida] in *La Prensa* (1928).

Cabildo abierto. Originally a formal mechanism to open dialogue between Spanish colonial officials and local citizens, the *Cabildo Abierto* of May 25, 1810, is the first entirely Argentine experiment in self-government. Viceroy Cisneros was asked to step down, meaning, in effect, the future Argentina would be independent.

Campo, Estanislao del (1834–1880). An Argentine poet who fought on the *Unitario* side in the Argentine civil wars. Author of *Fausto* (1860), about a gaucho who goes to Buenos Aires and attends a performance of Charles Gounod's *Faust*. He takes the opera as reality, and his account of it generates humor.

Caña. An alcoholic beverage derived from sugarcane.

Candombe. Drum-based Uruguayan music that originated in the black population. Combines African and tango elements.

Cané, Miguel (1851–1905). Argentine author of *Juvenilia* (1884), a memoir of student life. Cané's father (same name [1812–1863]) opposed Rosas.

Cansinos Assens, Rafael (1882–1964). Born in Seville, a poet and essayist who discovered his family's Jewish origins and converted to Judaism. Major influence on Borges in his youth and founder of Spanish *Ultraísmo*.

Carriego, Evaristo (1883–1912). A minor Buenos Aires poet, a friend of the Borges family. Author of *Misas herejes* [Heathen Masses] (1908). A denizen of Borges's neighborhood, Palermo, he is the subject of a 1930 biography by Borges.

Caseros. Battle (1852) that ended the dictatorship of Juan Manuel de Rosas. A coalition army composed of Argentines, Uruguayans, and Brazilians led by General Urquiza defeated Rosas's army and sent him into exile in England.

Cerro. Hill about four hundred feet in elevation across the bay from Montevideo.

Compadrito; andar quebrado. A thug handy with a knife, often a pimp and an "enforcer" for local political bosses. *Compadritos* were distinguished by their long, piled-up hair, their hats, and their high-heeled shoes. They affected a kind of bent-forward gait Borges mentions, *andar quebrado*.

Constitución. A Buenos Aires neighborhood about two kilometers from the city center. Site of the main railway station of the same name. President Irigoyen's home, sacked in the 1930 military coup, was in Constitución.

Corrales. Corrales Viejos, now Parque Patricio. A Buenos Aires neighborhood, birthplace of the tango.

Criollo, criollez, criollismo. A *criollo*, technically, is an Argentine of Spanish extraction. Borges claims *criollo* status and directs many of his essays (especially "The Complaint of All *Criollos*") to such people, but his grandmother, Fanny Haslam, was English. *Criollismo*, as practiced by Borges, is the almost anthropological intention to maintain the memory of *criollo* culture; *criollez* is simply another noun form of *criollismo*.

Cuchilla. A hill or series of steep hills. The term is usually associated with Uruguay.

Darío, Rubén (1867–1916). Pen name of Félix Rubén García Sarmiento, born in Nicaragua. Most important poet of the *Modernismo* movement (ca. 1880–1920). A major innovator both in verse and prose, despised by the avant-garde Borges as an author too tied to Europe and not sufficiently Spanish American. Darío, who lived in Buenos Aires, introduced Leopoldo Lugones to the Argentine reading public.

Diego, Gerardo (1896–1987). Spanish poet of the Generation of 1927.

Echeverría, Esteban (1805–1851). Introduced Romanticism to Argentine literature. An *unitario*, he wrote *El matadero* [The Slaughterhouse], published posthomously in 1871, as a satire against Juan Manuel de Rosas. It transcended propaganda and constitutes one of the foundation stones of Argentine literature.

Federales. Essentially, the spirit behind Juan Manuel de Rosas. Nominally, a belief in a loose confederation of Argentine provinces. Opposed to *unitarios*.

Fernández, Macedonio (1874–1952). Argentine author, friend of Borges's father and a mentor to Borges. An anarchic figure whose skewed vision of the universe added humor and irony to Borges's youthful solemnity.

Fernández Moreno, César (1919–1985). Argentine poet and essayist, son of Baldomero Fernández Moreno, also a poet.

Firpo, Luis Ángel (1894–1960). Argentine boxer. First Latin American to challenge for the world heavyweight title. Lost to Jack Dempsey, September 14, 1923.

Gálvez, Manuel (1882–1962). Argentine realist-naturalist novelist, author of *La maestra rural* [The Country Schoolteacher] (1914) and *El mal metafísico* [A Romantic Life] (1922). Wrote favorably about Juan Manuel de Rosas.

González Lanuza, Eduardo (1900–1984). Born in Spain, he was a full-fledged *Ultraísta* who, along with Borges, pasted copies of the mural magazine *Prisma* on the walls of Buenos Aires. Later abandoned avant-garde for traditional poetry.

Gringo. An impolite term used by Argentines in the nineteenth and early twentieth centuries to refer to foreigners, usually Italians.

Groussac, Paul (1848–1929). Born in France; moved to Buenos Aires in 1866. A historian and sardonic critic whose insults Borges includes in a 1933 article, "Arte de injuriar" [The Art of Verbal Abuse].

Güiraldes, Ricardo (1886–1927). Argentine author of the novel *Don Segundo Sombra* (1926), a haunting evocation of gaucho life. Güiraldes, though older than Borges, was a participant in the Buenos Aires avant-garde.

Gutiérrez, Eduardo (1851–1889). Argentine author of the novel *Juan Moreira*, spirited tale of gauchos.

Habanera. Cuban dance music, created circa 1878.

Hernández, José (1834–1886). Argentine poet, soldier, and politician, a *federal*. Author of *Martín Fierro* (1872)—a masterpiece of *poesía gauchesca,* often considered Argentina's epic—and *La vuelta de Martín Fierro* (1879), poetic attempts to call attention to the plight of the gaucho.

Herrera y Reissig, Julio (1875–1910). Uruguayan poet of the *Modernismo* movement. Author of *Los éxtasis de la montaña* [Ecstasies of the Mountain] (1904–7) and *Los peregrinos de piedra* [Pilgrims of Stone] (1909).

Hidalgo, Alberto (1897–1967). Peruvian poet who resided in Buenos Aires during the 1920s and "edited" an "oral magazine." Wrote, along with Borges and Huidobro, a prologue to the 1926 anthology of Spanish American avant-garde poetry, *Índice*.

Hidalgo, Bartolomé (1788–1822). Uruguayan poet, considered the founder of *poesía gauchesca*. Author of "Marcha Oriental" [Uruguayan March], the first patriotic song about Uruguay.

Hudson, William Henry (1841–1922). Anglo-Argentine author and naturalist. Author of *The Purple Land* (1885) and *El Ombú* (1902).

Huidobro, Vicente (1893–1948). Chilean poet, dramatist, and novelist. Inventor of "Creationism," his own theory of avant-garde poetry. Brought avant-garde techniques to the New World and was the first Spanish American to enter Hitler's bunker during the last days of World War II.

Ingenieros, José (1877–1925). Argentine sociologist and psychiatrist, professor of experimental psychology. A major figure in early twentieth-century Argentine science. His daughter, Cecilia, a dancer who trained with Martha Graham in New York, was Borges's girlfriend in the early 1940s.

Ipuche, Pedro Leandro (1889–1976). Uruguayan poet whose subject matter was the country and its people.

Irigoyen (Yrigoyen), Hipólito (1852–1933). Argentine politician, leader of Radical Party, president of Argentina 1916–1922, reelected 1928, removed from office by military coup led by General Uriburu.

Laforgue, Jules (1860–1887). French poet born in Montevideo. Known for wry humor and melancholy.

Liniers, Santiago de (1753–1810). French naval officer in the service of Spain, leader during Argentine expulsion of the English from Buenos Aires (see *Reconquista*). Named viceroy in 1807, he refused to recognize the governing Junta and was executed in Córdoba.

Linnig, Samuel (1888–1925). Born in Montevideo, spent most of his life in Buenos Aires. Minor poet, critic, and author of *sainetes* and several notable tangos, including "Milonguita," about a prostitute, and "Puente Alsina."

López, Vicente Fidel (1815–1903). Argentine historian and politician forced into exile by Rosas. Author of *La gran aldea* (1884), a novel depicting life in Buenos Aires.

Lugones, Leopoldo (1874–1938). Argentine poet, short-story writer, man of letters, and cultural critic. His early poetry, *Los crepúsculos del jardín* [Garden Twilights] (1905) and *Lunario sentimental* [Sentimental Lunar Calender] (1909), situated him at the forefront of second-generation *Modernismo*. His short stories show him to be an innovator, especially in the area of science fiction. Lugones began as a socialist but moved slowly to the center and then to the right. In 1924, at a celebration of the hundredth anniversary of the battle of Ayacucho (fought during the independence period), Lugones declared that the "hour of the sword" had returned and that military authority had to take power. His 1924 collection of love poems, *Romancero* [Ballads], was the object of a savage review by Borges, included here. Lugones committed suicide in 1938. Borges dedicated his 1960 book *El hacedor* to him.

Lunfardo. The jargon or semisecret language of the Buenos Aires underworld, infused with Italian turns of phrase or French terms (because of the French involvement in prostitution).

Mansilla, Lucio V. (1831–1913). Argentine general, author of *Una excursión a los indios ranqueles* [Expedition Against the Ranquel Indians] (1870).

Maples Arce, Manuel (1898–1981). Mexican poet and literary critic. Founder of *Estridentismo*. His poems are included in the 1926 anthology *Indice,* edited by Borges, Huidobro, and Hidalgo.

Maté. The gourd that holds the infusion of *hierba mate,* a kind of tea sipped through a straw. The written accent is superfluous and used merely to identify the drink and the special gourd.

Mazorca. After 1835, a secret police force used by Juan Manuel de Rosas to terrorize opponents. *Mazorca* means ear of corn, though many said it actually meant *más horca* (more gallows).

Milonga. A country song and a dance form.

Mocho, Fray. Pen name of José Sixto Álvarez (1858–1903), who wrote chronicles about life in Buenos Aires and authored *La vida de los ladrones célebres de Buenos Aires y sus maneras de robar* [Lives of the Celebrated Thieves of Buenos Aires and Their Techniques for Stealing] (1887) as well as *Memorias de un vigilante* [A Policeman's Memoirs] (1897).

Modernismo. A Spanish American literary movement, 1880–1920. *Modernismo* sought to renovate Spanish as a literary language, and to do so it incorporated elements from every European literary movement, from Romanticism to Decadentism. It includes such key figures as José Martí (Cuba), Rubén Darío (Nicaragua), and Leopoldo Lugones (Argentina).

Moreira, Juan. Protagonist of *Juan Moreira* (1879), a novel in gaucho style by Eduardo Gutiérrez.

Obligado, Rafael (1851–1920). Argentine author in gaucho style, who transformed Santos Vega, a *payador*, into a protagonist.

Ocho, asentada, media luna, paso atrás, cuerpeadas. Tango steps.

Ombú. A large tree of the evergreen family native to the Río de la Plata region. Borges uses it as a symbol of Uruguay.

Once, Plaza del. Located in Balvanera neighborhood, site of Our Lady of Balvanera church (1831). Zone around Avenida Corrientes is called Once after Plaza Once de Septiembre, alternate name of Plaza Miserere. Location of Bernardino Rivadavia's mausoleum. Macedonio Fernández lived in Balvanera and held court in Café Perla with Borges in attendance. A center of Jewish life in Buenos Aires.

Orillas, orillero. Low-class Buenos Aires neighborhoods and their inhabitants. The term *orillas* (shores or outskirts) is synonymous with *arrabal* or *suburbio*.

Palermo (Tierra del Fuego). Borges's childhood neighborhood; a poor district where Borges could see *compadritos*. Neighborhood of Evaristo Carriego.

Pampa. The flatlands south and west of Buenos Aires.

Parnasianism. A French poetic movement named for an anthology, *Le Parnasse contemporain* (1871–76). Art for art's sake. It includes such figures as Leconte de Lisle, Paul Verlaine, and Stéphane Mallarmé.

Payada. An improvised song sung to the accompaniment of a guitar. The singer, the *payador*, may compete with another in what is termed a *payada*. José Hernández's *Martín Fierro* contains a celebrated example.

Poesía gauchesca. Poetry, often satiric and political, written by educated poets in the vernacular of the gauchos during the Siege of Montevideo (1843–52) by the forces of Juan Manuel de Rosas. Bartolomé Hidalgo, Hilario Ascasubi, and Estanislao del Campo count among its founders, while José Hernández may be designated its master. Representative prose authors in this vein are Eduardo Gutiérrez (in the nineteenth century) and Ricardo Güiraldes (in the twentieth century).

Popham, Home Riggs (1762–1820). See *Reconquista*.

Porteño. A native of the city of Buenos Aires (the port), as opposed to a native of the province of Buenos Aires.

Portones. A series of decorative arches at the entry into the Palermo district of Buenos Aires. Their picture often appears on tourist postcards from the early years of the twentieth century. By the mid-1920s they were demolished.

Pulpería. Rural general store and social center where *truco* and other card games were played and *payadas* took place.

Quiroga, Facundo (1788–1835). The "Tiger of the Plains," a provincial warlord. He rejected the presidency of Rivadavia (1826). Though defeated several times, he became a national hero. Assassinated on February 16, 1835. Subject of a biography by Domingo Faustino Sarmiento, for whom Quiroga embodied Argentine barbarism.

Recoleta. Nineteenth-century cemetery in Recoleta district of Buenos Aires. Burial place of Eva Perón and location of Borges family mausoleum (Borges is buried in Geneva, Switzerland).

Reconquista (1806–1807). Invasion of Argentina by British forces under the command of Sir Home Riggs Popham. The successful Argentine force that expelled them was led by Santiago de Liniers (1753–1810). Liniers later refused to recognize the governing Junta and was shot in Córdoba.

Reyes, Alfonso (1889–1959). Mexican humanist, poet, literary critic, and diplomat—Mexican ambassador to Argentina in 1928, the year he met Borges. One of the towering figures of twentieth-century Spanish American culture and one of Borges's dear friends.

Roca, Julio Argentino (1843–1914). Argentine general and president (1880–86; 1898–1904). Fought in Triple Alliance war against Paraguay (1865–70) and suppressed Indians on frontier (1878–79).

Rojas, Ricardo (1882–1957). Argentine man of letters, rector of the University of Buenos Aires (1926–30), author of an eight-volume history of Argentine literature (ca. 1922). Often a target of Borges's irony.

Rosas, Juan Manuel de (1793–1877). Hero during Reconquista, he took over Federal Party after the death of Manuel Dorrego (1787–1828). Defeated Juan Lavalle (1797–1841) to become governor of Buenos Aires province (1829–32); led expedition against Indians. Reelected in 1835, he remained in power until his defeat at Caseros (1852). Went into exile in England.

Rosas, Prudencio (1800–1857). Argentine military figure, brother of Juan Manuel de Rosas, victor in 1839 battle Chascomús, which kept Juan Manuel in power.

Rossi, Vicente (1871–1945). Author of *Cosas de negros* [Black Matters] (1926), a pioneering study of African culture in the Río de la Plata. Borges reviewed Rossi's book in the magazine *Valoraciones* in 1926 and returned to it in "Genealogy of the Tango," included here.

Saavedra, Cornelio (1759–1829). Argentine military and political leader. Hero of defense of Buenos Aires against the English, he also participated in the May Revolution and was president of governing Junta (1810).

Sainete. Term derives from farce, a Spanish comic opera. In Argentina it uses vernacular subjects, low life.

San Martín, José de (1778–1850). Argentine general, leader of independence movement. Fought against Napoleon in Spain, returned to Argentina, led army in liberation of Chile (after battles of Chacabuco and Maipú in 1818). After meeting with Simón Bolívar at Guayaquil (Ecuador) in 1822, resigned and moved to France.

Santos Vega. A legendary *payador* used as a character by Bartolomé Mitre, Hilario Ascasubi, and Rafael Obligado. Eduardo Gutiérrez wrote a novel about him.

Saravia, Aparicio (1856–1904). Uruguayan warlord born in Brazil. Supposedly participated in Revolution of the Lances (1870–72), rose up again in 1904, and was fatally wounded at Masoller. His death brought stability to Uruguay.

Sarmiento, Domingo Faustino (1811–1888). A member of the *unitario* party, he opposed Juan Manuel de Rosas, who forced him into Chilean exile. Championed public education; at the side of Urquiza at the battle of Caseros. Biographer of Juan Facundo Quiroga, *Civilization or Barbarism: Life of Juan Facundo Quiroga* (1845). President of Argentina in 1868.

Schiaffino, Eduardo (1858–1935). Argentine painter and critic.

Sicardi, Francisco (1856–1927). Argentine writer and physician. Documented the misery of Buenos Aires in his *Libro extraño* [Strange Book] (1894–1902), a novel of naturalist tendency.

Silva Valdés, Fernán (1887–1975). Uruguayan poet who moved away from *Modernismo* to nativism, *criollo* themes. Wrote *Poemas nativos* (1925); also wrote lyrics for tangos and *milongas*.

Suburbio. A poor neighborhood in an outlying district. The term is synonymous with *arrabal* and *orillas*.

Tallon, José Sebastián (1904–1954). Caricaturist linked to socially concerned authors of Boedo group. Wrote children's poetry.

Tejedor, Carlos (1817–1903). Argentine politician, staunch defender of Buenos Aires. In governments of Bartolomé, Mitre, and Sarmiento. Led insurrection in 1880 and was defeated. Author of Argentine penal code. Song about him is sung when one holds a triumphant hand in *truco*.

Torre, Guillermo de (1900–1971). Poet and critic, born in Spain. Participated in *Ultraísmo* and married Borges's sister Norah in 1928.

Truco. A card game played in Argentina, Uruguay, and Brazil. In Argentina, the *truco* deck consists of forty cards, with no 8's, 9's, or jokers. It may be played by two, four, or six players. There are three cards in a hand, and three hands in a round, with the winning player or team winning two out of three. The first player or team to reach thirty points wins. A *truco* (trick) won gives a point to the winning player or team. *Envido* is the highest combination of two cards in the same suit or a single high card. *Flor* means having all three cards of the same suit. If a player says *Truco*, he raises the value of the hand to two points. The opposition may accept by saying *Quiero* or decline by saying *No quiero*. *Envido* is said before play begins and takes precedence over the *truco* point count. *Truco* is a game of deception, with players engaging in tricky conversation with one another to create distractions and to communicate with team members. Borges published a poem on *truco* in his first book of poems, *Fervor de Buenos Aires* (1923). He repeats phrases from the poem in this essay.

Ultraísmo. Spanish avant-garde movement launched by Rafael Cansinos Assens in 1918 as a reaction against *Modernismo*. Borges was deeply involved with Spanish *Ultraísmo* and brought it to Buenos Aires, where he and his friends promulgated it in two magazines: *Prisma* (1921–22), a mural magazine pasted to walls, and *Proa* (1922–23), a conventional magazine. Borges published an article in *Nosotros* in 1921, listing the attributes of *Ultraísta* poetry, stressing the importance of metaphor, the banishing of sentiment, the use of free verse, neologism, and typographical innovations. A difference between Argentine and Spanish *Ultraísmo* is the former's *criollismo*.

Unamuno, Miguel de (1864–1936). Member of Spanish Generation of 1898, a philosopher of metaphysical cast and a staunch defender of Spanish tradition. Corresponded with Borges.

Unitarios. The opposition to the dictatorship of Juan Manuel de Rosas, the *unitarios* nominally favored a strong central government.

Urquiza, Justo José de (1801–1870). Wealthy landowner; in 1842, a general under Rosas. A *federal*, he turned against Rosas and defeated him at the Battle of Caseros in 1852. Assassinated by minor warlord López Jordán.

Venteveo. *Pitangus sulfuratus* (*Linnaeus*); the Great Kiskadee, a passerine bird with a bright yellow chest.

Wilde, Eduardo (1844–1913). Humorous, ironic prose author.

Wilde, José Antonio (1813–1887). Physician. Served with Urquiza at Caseros, where Rosas's army was defeated in 1852. Later highly active in public health and education.

Wilkins, John (1614–1672). Author of *An Essay Towards a Real Character and a Philosophical Language* (1668), an attempt to design a universal language for "natural philosophers."

Zaguán. In traditional South American architecture, an entryway into a house. The *zaguán* leads to the patio.

Sources

Below is a list of sources indicating where each piece was originally published, other than in volumes that give their names to the sections in this collection.

From *A Universal History of Iniquity*
[*Historia universal de la infamia,* 1935]

Man on Pink Corner
"Hombre de la esquina rosada": definitive version published in *Historia universal de la infamia* (1935). Earlier versions: "Leyenda policial," in *Martín Fierro* (1927), and "Hombres pelearon," in *El idioma de los argentinos* (1928).

From *Inquisitions*
[*Inquisiciones,* 1925]

Buenos Aires
"Buenos Aires," *Cosmópolis,* 1921.

The Mythical Founding of Buenos Aires
"Fundación mítica de Buenos Aires," *Cuaderno San Martín,* 1929.

Ascasubi
"Ascasubi," no earlier publication.

The *Criollo* Element in Ipuche
"La criolledad en Ipuche," *Proa,* 1924.

The Complaint of All *Criollos*
"Queja de todo criollo," no earlier publication.

Eduardo González Lanuza
"E. González Lanuza," *Proa,* 1924.

From *Moon Across the Way*
[*Luna de enfrente*, 1925]

General Quiroga Rides to His Death in a Carriage
"El General Quiroga va en coche al muere," *Luna de enfrente*, 1925.

From *The Full Extent of My Hope*
[*El tamaño de mi esperanza*, 1926]

Carriego and the Meaning of the *Arrabal*
"Carriego y el significado del arrabal," *La Prensa*, 1926.

The Full Extent of My Hope
"El tamaño de mi esperanza," *Valoraciones*, March, 1926.

The Pampa and the *Suburbio* Are Gods
"La pampa y el suburbia son dioses," *Proa*, 1926.

The Purple Land
"La tierra cárdena," *Proa*, 1925.

Leopoldo Lugones: *Romancero*
"Leopoldo Lugones: Romancero," *Inicial*, 1926.

From *The Language of the Argentines*
[*El idioma de los argentinos*, 1928]

Truco
"Truco," *La Prensa*, 1928.
"Truco," *Fervor de Buenos Aires*, 1923.

Genealogy of the Tango
"Ascendencias del tango," *Martín Fierro*, 1927.

Situating Almafuerte
"Ubicación de Almafuerte," *La Prensa*, 1927.

The Language of the Argentines
"El idioma de los argentinos," lecture at the Instituto Popular
   de Conferencias, 1927.

From *Evaristo Carriego*, 1930

Buenos Aires: Palermo

A History of the Tango
"Historia del tango," first published as such in the 1955 edition of
   Evaristo Carriego.

Miscellany, 1931–51

Our Inabilities
"Nuestras imposibilidades," *Sur*, 1931.

I, a Jew
"Yo, judío," *Megáfono*, n. 12, 1934.

Borges's Prologue to the German Edition of Enrique Amorim's
   La carreta, 1937.

Definition of a Germanophile
"Definición de germanófilo," *El Hogar,* 1940.

Our Poor Individualism
"Nuestro pobre individualismo," *Sur*, 1946.

The Argentine Writer and Tradition
"El escritor argentine y la tradición," lecture delivered at the Colegio
   Libre de Estudios Superiores, Dec. 19, 1951.

From *Fictions*
[*Ficciones,* 1944]

The South
"El sur" *La Nación*, 1953.

ALSO AVAILABLE FROM PENGUIN CLASSICS

General Editor: Suzanne Jill Levine

ISBN 978-0-14-310572-5

On Writing

Edited with an Introduction and
Notes by Suzanne Jill Levine

Featuring many pieces appearing
in English for the first time—
including Borges's groundbreaking
essay on magical realism, "Stories
from Turkenstan"—here is a
master class in the art of writing
by one of its most distinguished
and innovative practitioners.

ISBN 978-0-14-310569-5

On Mysticism

Edited with an Introduction by
Maria Kodama

Presented here for the first time
in any language is a collection
of Borges's essays, fiction, and
poetry exploring the role of the
mysterious and spiritual in his life
and work.

PENGUIN CLASSICS

Printed in the United States
by Baker & Taylor Publisher Services